ACT For Treating Children

The Essential Guide To Acceptance And Commitment Therapy For Kids

Tamar D. Black, PhD

16pt

Read How You Want
LARGE PRINT BOOKS, BRAILLE & DAISY

Copyright Page from the Original Book

New Harbinger Publications is an employee-owned company

NEW HARBINGER PUBLICATIONS is a registered trademark of New Harbinger Publications, Inc.

Copyright © 2022 by Tamar D. Black
New Harbinger Publications, Inc.
5674 Shattuck Avenue
Oakland, CA 94609
www.newharbinger.com

All Rights Reserved

Cover design by Amy Daniel

Illustrations by Gila Bloch

Acquired by Tesilya Hanauer

Edited by Rona Bernstein

Indexed by James Minkin

Library of Congress Cataloging-in-Publication Data on file

TABLE OF CONTENTS

"A beautifully written and comprehensive book that addresses every aspect of the use of acceptance and commitment therapy (ACT) methods with children. In addition to putting forth a treasure trove of new materials and new ideas, I love how it builds out classic ACT methods in ways that are thoroughly age-appropriate and yet recognizable, so that practitioners can follow Tamar's lead and begin to apply other things they may know about ACT in creative new ways as well. A transformational book that every practitioner who works with children should have at arm's reach."

—**Steven C. Hayes, PhD,** Nevada Foundation Professor in the department of psychology at the University of Nevada, Reno; and originator of ACT

"Tamar Black wrote *ACT for Treating Children* to be the book she wished was available when she first started using ACT with children. She has created a book that is an absolute must, not just for clinicians new to ACT, but also experienced ACT therapists. This book is highly informative, full of clinical tips and practical advice, and is an interesting read from start to finish. Highly recommended!"

—**Kirk Strosahl, PhD,** cofounder of ACT, and coauthor of *The Mindfulness and Acceptance Workbook for Depression*

"In this fascinating and important book, Tamar Black guides practitioners through how to help children gain insight into their minds and cultivate competencies that can promote well-being. Especially helpful are its extensive and clear descriptions of experiential work. Even if you are not an ACT therapist, the wealth of ideas is clearly written, easily understood, and of immense value. Anyone working with children will gain enormously from this book."
—**Paul Gilbert, OBE,** founder of compassion-focused therapy (CFT), and author of *The Compassionate Mind*

"*ACT for Treating Children* is a clear, thorough, and deeply pragmatic guide for applying ACT with children. The book contains a wealth of clinical experience, getting into the nuances of how to utilize ACT with children in a way that anticipates and answers common questions that clinicians are likely to have! An excellent resource for all therapists who work with children."
—**Russell Kolts,** professor of psychology at Eastern Washington University, and author of *CFT Made Simple* and *The Compassionate-Mind Guide to Managing Your Anger*

"What a wonderful book! As an experienced supervisor and trainer of ACT, I was deeply impressed by how adeptly Tamar Black has keyed into frequent points of confusion and misunderstanding. This book is both a phenomenal introduction to ACT and its therapeutic stance, as well as the book I always wish I had to share with child psychologists in training. The clear guidance on conceptualization and child-appropriate questions for assessment are bright spots throughout."

—**Matthew D. Skinta, PhD, ABPP,** assistant professor of psychology at Roosevelt University, and author of *Contextual Behavior Therapy for Sexual and Gender Minority Clients*

"This book has great practical application, with easy-to-understand descriptions of developmentally appropriate case conceptualization, technique, and stance. There are wonderful examples, including a helpful section on working with parents. The accompanying worksheets help concretize metaphor and experiential exercises, which is essential for this age group. This protocol-like book will be very useful for individuals new to ACT or new to ACT with youth. I highly recommend it!"

—**Amy R. Murrell, PhD,** licensed psychologist, peer-reviewed ACT trainer, ACBS fellow, author of the Becca Epps series, and coauthor of *The Joy of Parenting*

"This is a wonderfully practical book—from the delightful *Kidflex* to worksheets to important suggestions that will make anyone a better therapist with any client. This book will be a lifesaver for people wading into doing ACT with kids. It is truly an essential guide for anyone wishing to bring ACT to their work with children, and for seasoned ACT clinicians who want to hone their craft."

—Christopher McCurry, PhD, author of *Parenting Your Anxious Child with Mindfulness and Acceptance,* and coauthor of *The Mindfulness and Acceptance Workbook for Teen Anxiety*

"A long-overdue and much-needed book, *ACT For Treating Children* provides a step-by-step *Kidflex* model for teaching the heart of ACT to children in an approachable, compassionate, and very helpful way. If you work with children, you need this wonderful book."

—Janina Scarlet, PhD, award-winning author of *Superhero Therapy*

"In *ACT for Treating Children,* Tamar Black provides a refreshing adaptation of ACT to the complex work of psychotherapy with kids. Tamar Black brings substantial clinical experience to bear in accessible theoretical adaptations to the psychological flexibility model, immediately actionable technologies, and easy-to-follow guidelines for the therapist's stance—all with well-contextualized examples. Reading this book

will benefit any child therapist interested in doing transformative work with children."
—**Emily K. Sandoz, PhD,** professor of psychology at the University of Louisiana at Lafayette, and coauthor of *The Mindfulness and Acceptance Workbook for Bulimia*

"Written by an expert on ACT, Tamar Black, *ACT for Treating Children* provides an all-inclusive guide on how to implement ACT with children. This book fills a void in the ACT literature. Reading this book greatly expanded my ACT repertoire, and it will do the same for you."
—**Michael P. Twohig, PhD,** professor at Utah State University, and coauthor of *ACT in Steps*

"At last, not just a guide to ACT for children, but a comprehensive, straightforward, and fun one at that!"
—**Christopher Willard, PsyD,** faculty at Harvard Medical School, and author of *Growing Up Mindful*

In memory of my cousin Monty Meyer, who inspired me to become a child psychologist the first time we met when I was twelve years old.

Acknowledgments

I wish to acknowledge the Boonwurrung people of the Kulin Nation as the Traditional Owners and Custodians of the land on which I reside, work, and wrote this book. I pay my respects to their Elders past, present, and emerging, and acknowledge and uphold their continuing relationship to this land.

To the incredible team at New Harbinger Publications, thank you so much, especially Tesilya Hanauer for your enthusiasm about this book and your guidance, support, and assistance, along with Clancy Drake, Madison Davis, Caleb Beckwith, Amy Shoup, and Analis Souza. To freelance editors Rona Bernstein and Gretel Hakanson, thank you so much for all of your encouragement, efforts, and patience. Thank you to Julian McNally for providing feedback on this book and for your encouragement. To Gila Bloch, thank you so much for drawing the images for the worksheets, and for your creativity and intuition.

To Steve Hayes, Kirk Strosahl, and Kelly Wilson, on a personal and professional level, thank you so much for creating ACT, which has greatly enriched my life—if I didn't use ACT in my own life, I wouldn't have had the courage to write this book.

To Amy Murrell and Lisa Coyne, thank you for leading the way in using ACT with children and parents and for encouraging and supporting me. Thank you to Louise Hayes for taking me on as your first PhD student and for all that you have taught me.

Thank you to everyone in the ACT and compassion-focused communities whom I've learned so much from and have been greatly inspired by.

To the children and parents I work with, who inspire and amaze me with their courage, determination, and willingness, thank you for allowing me to be a part of your journey.

To my best friend and husband, Gavin, thank you for your endless love and encouragement, for your practical and moral support, and for always believing in me. To my children, Sara and Ariella, thank you for your enthusiasm about this book and for always cheering for me. To my parents, Ruth and David, thank you for having encouraged and supported my dream of becoming a child psychologist since I was twelve years old, and for fostering my love of listening to, talking to, and helping others.

Foreword

I must confess, I'm not a big fan of writing forewords, and earlier this year, I swore that I wasn't going to do anymore. But when Tamar Black reached out to me, I couldn't say no. Well, I suppose I could have—but I didn't want to because I was so excited when she told me what this book was about.

I can't tell you how delighted I am that we have finally, at long last, gotten a book of this nature. I've been hoping for years that someone would write a really practical, simple, and comprehensive book on ACT for kids—and I'm pleased to say that this one truly fits the bill. Tamar is a world-renowned expert on using ACT with children, and she's done an excellent job of spelling out how we adapt and modify ACT for working flexibly with children aged five to twelve. (We also live in the same city, and I've known her for many years, so I have often recommended that friends take their kids to her.)

What's great about this book is that even if you know nothing about ACT, it will give you a rapid grounding in the basics. Pretty much anyone doing therapy with kids will benefit, and will easily be able to put these skills into practice and use them in conjunction with other models. On the other hand, if you already know how to use ACT with adults or adolescents, you'll find this book a treasure trove, full of ideas and strategies for effectively adapting the way you work.

Let's face it: many therapists get stuck trying to do ACT with children. Some find themselves doing it in a formulaic way: always following the same sequence, sticking to the same metaphors and exercises. Some try simply to translate "adult ACT" into children's language—whereupon they quickly discover that kids either don't get it or don't like it. Some fall into classic ACT therapist traps such as "talking about ACT" (discussing ACT concepts and ideas instead of actually doing the essential experiential work) or "metaphor abuse" (bombarding clients with an endless stream of metaphors in the hope that one will make a difference). And all too many do exercises or set homework tasks that are developmentally inappropriate—a sure recipe for failure.

If these things have ever happened to you, you may have felt a bit despondent or frustrated. But the good news is, Tamar will show you how to avoid all these pitfalls (or get yourself back out after you've fallen in) and instead, work fluently and flexibly with young clients. She'll teach you how to dance around the "ACT Kidflex" and make your sessions playful, creative, and effective. You'll learn how to do the experiential work of ACT, and keep your clients engaged as you do so. And very importantly, you'll discover how to tailor your interventions so that they are developmentally appropriate!

So if you want to be effective and creative in helping kids live by their values, face their fears, unhook from difficult thoughts, make room for difficult feelings, develop self-compassion, act effectively, and engage fully in life, you've come to the right place. This book will give you all the knowledge you need to achieve those ends. Enjoy the journey!

—Russ Harris
Melbourne, August 29, 2021

CHAPTER I

An Overview of Using ACT to Treat Children

This book is written for psychiatrists, psychologists, counselors, school psychologists, school counselors, therapists, and students who provide individual therapy to children aged five to twelve years, and those who wish to learn how. I've purposely written this as a very practical book, a "how to" guide for working with children using acceptance and commitment therapy (ACT)—a brief, individual therapy approach—in a developmentally appropriate way. The book caters to therapists with a broad range of experience, from those with no prior knowledge of or training in ACT to highly experienced, expert ACT therapists.

What You'll Learn in This Book

If you have already used ACT with children, you might have noticed that you usually start therapy at the same place with each child, following the same intervention plan, and using the same exercises. Or, you might think that using ACT with children is the same as using ACT with adolescents and adults, but you often realize that the child doesn't understand what you are saying, or doesn't participate much in sessions. You might find yourself doing most of the talking, and using ACT metaphor after metaphor, resulting in the child simply agreeing with you rather than disclosing their struggles. It might also be challenging to know how to suggest developmentally appropriate home tasks, for both the child and their parents or caregivers, to reinforce what you have done in sessions. Finally, the child might be bored in sessions, not completing the suggested home tasks, or reluctant to return. By reading this book, you'll learn how to avoid these pitfalls and optimize your ACT sessions with children. And whether you're experienced in or new to ACT, this book will provide you with practical information and tools to enable you to deliver ACT effectively with your young clients.

This chapter will provide a brief introduction to ACT, an overview of how we modify ACT for use with children, and some important pointers to keep in mind when conducting ACT sessions with children.

In chapter 2, you'll learn about the first session with the child, including how to use a case conceptualization template developed especially for use with children and their parents, with detailed suggestions of how to ask each question. We will also look at how to introduce ACT to children, invite them to become their own superhero, and give them a voice in the therapeutic process.

In chapter 3, you will start learning about how to use the processes of what I call the ACT Kidflex, a model adapted from the ACT Hexaflex, which involves six processes to help clients achieve psychological flexibility. Chapter 3 will focus on two of these processes: *let it be* and *let it go*. In chapter 4, we'll focus on the ACT processes *choose what matters* and *do what matters*, and then in chapter 5 we'll learn about the remaining two processes: *stay here* and *notice yourself*. Chapter 6 introduces us to ACT's best friend, *be kind and caring to yourself*, and focuses on how to teach this vital skill to children using exercises in sessions. In this way, children can experience what being kind and caring to themselves looks and feels like. In chapter 7, we will learn how to work with parents of younger children, without doing therapy with their child. Then we'll conclude in chapter 8 with some final tips for how to start using what you've learned in this book.

The chapters in this book, beginning with chapter 3, feature an extensive list of highly experiential exercises (*experiential* refers to something that's experienced, as opposed to having a discussion about a concept or idea) that you can do in sessions with children. Using these exercises with your young clients will enable them to build a coping toolkit to help them cope with stress and manage difficult thoughts and feelings. You will also find case examples, which include suggestions for home tasks for the child to practice in between sessions, as well as home tasks for the parent to reinforce what the child has learned in sessions. All exercises are purposely simple so as to be developmentally appropriate for children and easy for you to implement, and the wide range of exercises will allow you to choose what best suits the needs and personalities of the children you work with.

HELPFUL HINT

As emphasized in this book, a cornerstone of successful ACT with kids is involving the child in the therapeutic process by doing exercises *with*—rather than *to*—the child and also having some fun.

Worksheets are provided in chapters 3 through 6 and are available for download in color at the website for this book: http://www.newhar binger.com/49760. (See the very back of this book for more details.) You can use the worksheets in sessions with children, and you can also give them to parents for their child to do under their supervision at home. Some of the worksheets are repeats of exercises in the chapters, enabling the child to have a visual of the exercise to take home with them, while other worksheets introduce new material. Based on what you think will be helpful for the child, you can choose whether to use all of the worksheets with the same child or select one or several. Additional materials, including the case conceptualization template and exercise scripts, are also available for download.

Finally, when you finish reading this book, head over to the book's website, http://www.ne wharbinger.com/49760, where you'll find an extended case protocol of treatment I provided to an eight-year-old client in six sessions. I'll take you through each session one at a time, showing you in detail how I used ACT. Each process of the ACT Kidflex—along with *be kind and caring to yourself*—is addressed, including the exercises conducted and home tasks recommended for both the child and her parents.

Note that all of the exercises, worksheets, questions, home tasks, and recommendations in the book are also applicable to caregivers with whom the child resides.

Introduction to Acceptance and Commitment Therapy (ACT)

Before we get started in learning how to use ACT (Hayes, Strosahl, et al., 1999, 2012) with children, I'll provide a short introduction to ACT and a description of how it differs from cognitive behavioral therapy (CBT; Beck et al., 1979). If you are familiar with ACT, this will be a review. Following this, I'll introduce you to the new ACT Kidflex, a behavioral model for using ACT with children aged five to twelve years, including a description of each of its processes along with examples. Then we'll look at the ACT stance and how you can use it in sessions.

If this is the first time you are learning about ACT, I encourage you to also explore the multitude of theoretical resources available to increase your understanding of ACT, such as:

- *ACT Made Simple* (Harris, 2009)
- *ACT Made Simple, 2nd edition* (Harris, 2019)
- *Learning ACT* (Luoma et al., 2007)

ACT (pronounced as the word "act," not as A-C-T) has its roots in applied behavior analysis (ABA; Baer et al., 1968) and relational frame theory (RFT; Hayes et al., 2001), which is a theoretical approach to language and cognition. ACT is also based on the philosophy of functional contextualism (Biglan & Hayes, 1996; Hayes, 1993; Hayes et al., 1988), which holds that all behavior is designed to serve the best interests of the organism. That is, to be "understood" from a clinical perspective, a behavior must be considered in the context in which it occurs. The inner world of language and thought, even awareness itself, must be considered as a context that can initiate, reinforce, and shape a set of behaviors. From a functional contextual perspective, the most effective way to change behavior is by manipulating the contextual factors—such as what a person has learned and their language processes—that maintain the behavior (Coyne et al., 2011).

To understand ACT, it's important to know the differences between ACT and CBT and have a basic introduction to relational frame theory. We'll cover these topics below.

How Is ACT Different from CBT?

ACT and CBT both utilize behavioral techniques. However, the models differ in their theoretical approach, the change processes (i.e., mechanisms that lead to change) involved, and how the two therapies address language and cognition. ACT focuses less on the content of private experiences (thoughts, emotions, feelings, memories, urges, physical sensations, and behaviors) than CBT does; rather, the therapist using ACT helps the person form a detached, nonreactive relationship to these private experiences.

CBT approaches tend to view the content of distressing and unwanted thoughts, emotions, feelings, or memories as something clients need to evaluate and restructure to be more consistent with a logical analysis of the situation. The term "personal scientist" has often been used to describe this core underlying philosophy of the CBT approach. Whereas CBT emphasizes changing clients' thoughts and behavior with the goal of symptom reduction, ACT emphasizes openness and acceptance of all psychological events (such as thoughts, emotions, feelings, memories, and behaviors) without doing anything to change, avoid, or limit them, despite their type and label given. The therapist using ACT focuses on how a person's behavioral responses work for them in terms of identified values or life goals (Coyne et al., 2011).

Relational Frame Theory

Relational frame theory (RFT) is focused on the origin of verbal abilities and is based on the notion that human language and cognition are dependent on contextual cues known as *relational frames*. Humans relate experiences such as feeling an emotion, having a thought, or seeing or smelling something to social conventions, therefore deriving their own meaning of these experiences—a process known as *arbitrary contextual control* (Luoma et al., 2007). In RFT, this is a *learned operant behavior* (an operant behavior is anything a person does that they can increase or decrease, for example, contacting friends, asking for help, and withdrawing from others).

RFT and ACT take the perspective that when language and cognitions are rigid, people tend to live in ways that are psychologically inflexible, and as a result psychopathology frequently develops (Luoma et al., 2007). For example, a twelve-year-old girl might have the thought *I feel so guilty about having given in to* peer pressure to drink alcohol at the party, but I cannot tell my parents because they will think badly of me. Having a close relationship with her parents is important to her, but she strongly believes they will judge her and lose respect for her if she tells them she drank alcohol. She fears that her parents will find out, and as a result, she develops anxiety. The ACT approach with this girl would be to (1) use strategies that teach her to let go of her attachment to her thoughts about the party and disrupt unhelpful verbal strategies and (2) encourage her to sit with her feelings of guilt and inform her parents in the service of furthering a close relationship with them.

Is ACT Suitable for Children?

Several studies have found ACT to be effective for children. Fang and Ding's (2020) meta-analysis of seven randomized controlled trials of ACT with children up to age twelve years found that ACT significantly reduced anxiety and depression in children and was equivalent to CBT in effectiveness. A review by Swain et al. (2015) showed that for children aged twelve years and under, three studies found ACT to be significantly effective; one of these studies was a randomized controlled trial.

Children often respond very well to ACT and usually enjoy the interactive and experiential nature of the therapeutic techniques. Rather than resembling a class at school where teaching is frequently didactic and might require children to sit and listen quietly to the teacher, ACT sessions with children involve both the child and therapist engaging in exercises together (this will be discussed in greater detail in chapters 3, 4, and 5).

HELPFUL HINT

The way that I use ACT with children is really simple. When I provide explanations, I ensure that I use plain, easy-to-understand language, and I make the exercises as uncomplicated as possible. In fact, I've noticed that the way I use ACT with children gets more and more simple over time.

After giving explanations and instructions, I say something to the child like "If there's anything I said that's at all confusing or doesn't make sense, please let me know, and I'll find another way to explain it." This is because the child might not feel comfortable telling you that they don't understand what you are talking about unless you explicitly ask.

Sometimes when I'm in a session with a child of, say, five to ten years old, I think of an exercise that I'd like to use but that I might not have tried with someone as young as the child. Or, I might have attended an ACT workshop on working with adults and learned a great new exercise, or read about an exercise in a book that's written for using ACT with adults, and I'd really love to try to adapt it for use with children. To do this, I try to make the exercise *much* easier for children to understand. This might sound daunting for you, particularly if you are new to working with children, or new to using ACT with children. It was also daunting for me when I first began trying to work out how to use ACT with children: I worried that the child would be too young to understand the concepts and that I might not be able to do the exercises correctly. I encourage you to be willing to try and have a go, even if your mind tells you that you aren't certain that the child is old enough for the particular exercise. If the child doesn't understand the exercise, you could try making it less complicated. One technique that's helped me to work out whether I have adapted an exercise sufficiently is to ask myself whether the exercise will be easy for the child to remember. If you aren't sure how to make an exercise less complicated, you could try another exercise that addresses the same ACT process.

When working with younger children (say five to eight years old), particularly if they are very mature for their age, I know that sometimes I can mistakenly use language that's too old for them. As a result of being aware of this, I tell younger children—before discussing any concepts or providing explanations and instructions—that sometimes I might forget how old they are and think I'm sitting in my therapy room with an older child. I ask them to let me know if I do use language that's too old for them so that I can change the words I use to be suitable for them. I've noticed that children seem to like the fact that I'm willing to admit that I may make errors: being able to admit my own vulnerability and flaws shows children (and their parents) that I don't consider myself perfect and am open to and accepting of feedback. This demonstrates my *own* flexibility and detachment from my own story about who I am. (By "story," I mean a way of describing ourselves, which in ACT is called the *conceptualized self* as well as *self-as-content.*) This willingness on my part helps me to build rapport with both children and their parents.

ACT can be very helpful for children because it focuses on increasing acceptance, which can build self-esteem and resilience and improve quality of life. This book was written to help you develop the skills to equip children to improve their mental health and resilience and overcome disorders such as anxiety and depression. Children, like adolescents and adults, can also struggle to bounce back from difficulties; ACT teaches them very important life skills using strategies that are applicable to a wide range of disorders and can be applied to other challenges in the future.

ACT can also help children to regulate and manage difficult emotions and cope with the ups and downs of life. This will help your clients become more empowered and confident to self-manage their difficulties and be less controlled by and fearful of their thoughts and feelings. The strategies are practical and easy to implement, and the child will be able to use them by themself, discreetly, and in multiple environments, such as at home, in school, and in social and leisure activities.

Let's take a look now at the ACT Kidflex, its processes, and how it's used with children.

The ACT Kidflex

The ACT model of behavior change (Hayes et al., 2006) is commonly referred to as the "ACT Hexaflex." This model consists of six core ACT processes: *acceptance, defusion, values, committed action, contact with the present moment, and selfas-context.* These processes aim to build *psychological flexibility,* which is defined as "the ability to contact the present moment more fully as a conscious human being, and to change or persist in behavior when doing so serves valued ends" (Hayes et al., 2006, p.7).

I adapted the ACT model of behavior change to create the ACT Kidflex (shown in the figure on the next page) in order to make it developmentally appropriate for children, using language they can understand. As such, the six core processes of the ACT Kidflex are *let it be, let it go, choose what matters, do what matters, stay here,* and *notice yourself.* In the ACT Kidflex, psychological flexibility is termed *I am flexible*, which can be defined as "stay here, notice what's happening without trying to change your thoughts or feelings, and keep going or change your actions when needed, to do what matters to you." In the Kidflex model, you can see how *I am flexible* is represented by the six points of the hexagon.

Let's consider how you could use the ACT Kidflex with a child. Imagine working with a child who enjoys learning to play piano. The child wants to play at their first piano recital because they feel proud of how much they have achieved, but as the day of the recital approaches, they avoid practicing piano for fear of experiencing anxiety about not performing well. An ACT approach would be to ask the child if there was anything about the piano recital that was important to them (*choose what matters*). You could then encourage the child to practice piano while noticing what they're feeling and where they feel it the strongest in their body (*stay here*) without trying to do anything to reduce feeling anxious (*let it be*), saying hi to thoughts of messing up during the recital when they show up (*let it go*), watching themself having those thoughts (*notice yourself*), and continuing to practice even in the presence of those thoughts (*do what matters*). Let's look at each process, including examples of how to use it with children.

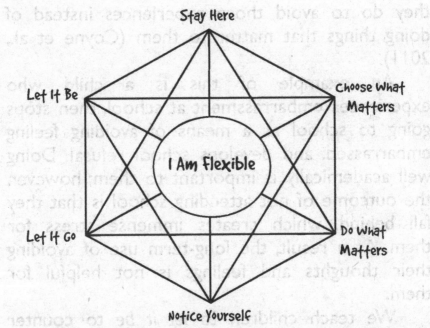

The ACT Kidflex (Adapted from Hayes et al., 2006)

Let It Be

Let it be refers to letting unwanted private experiences (such as thoughts, feelings, emotions, memories, urges, physical sensations, and behaviors) just be there, without trying to do anything with them, like get rid of them, avoid them, replace them, or look for evidence for and against them. There are some situations where not letting it be can be helpful short term, for example, listening to music as a means of distraction to get through having a shot or blood test. However, not letting it be is unhelpful long term if a person focuses more on not having certain private experiences and restricts what they do to avoid those experiences instead of doing things that matter to them (Coyne et al., 2011).

An example of this is a child who experiences embarrassment at school, then stops going to school as a means of avoiding feeling embarrassed, and develops school refusal. Doing well academically is important to them; however, the outcome of not attending school is that they fall behind, which creates immense stress for them. As a result, the long-term use of avoiding their thoughts and feelings is not helpful for them.

We teach children to *let it be* to counter the toxic effects of being stuck with their thoughts and following rigid rules they have developed that govern their own behavior, in order to avoid private experiences. For example, a child attended a party where they felt excluded by the other children, resulting in their feeling lonely and sad during the party. As a result of their experience, they developed a rule of "I don't go to parties because no one ever wants to talk to me." By teaching the child the ACT process *let it be*, they can learn to do things that matter to them (Hayes et al., 2006), even if they experience discomfort while doing so.

Using the earlier example of the child who was worried about their piano recital, an ACT approach of using *let it be* would be to suggest that they try to let their thoughts about not performing well just be, without trying to do anything with them, and when they become aware that these thoughts are present, they gently bring their attention back to the task of practicing piano. In this way, ACT aims to foster *let it be* while pursuing things that matter, instead of trying to regulate emotions or reduce symptoms (Coyne et al., 2011).

Let It Go

Let it go refers to stepping back and getting some separation between us and our thoughts so that we are not stuck with or attached to them. We are not trying to get rid of our thoughts, or reduce how often they show up, or replace them; rather, *let it go* involves being able to see them for what they are—just thoughts—without letting them have lots of power over us. When I introduce *let it go* to children, I begin by explaining that thoughts start off as letters of the alphabet, then our minds put the letters together to make words, which become sentences. I then tell them that just because our minds come up with these sentences, it does not mean that they're always true, or that we always have to believe everything our mind tells us.

For example, the child who was having thoughts of not performing well in their piano recital might use *let it go* by saying to themself, *I am having the thought that I will not do well in my piano recital* or *My mind is telling me I will not do well* instead of *I will not do well in my piano recital.* This encourages them to see their feelings and thoughts as just feelings and thoughts (Barnes-Holmes et al., 2004) rather than believing that what their mind is telling them is something that's absolutely true and that they must believe and listen to (and therefore stop practicing for the recital because they know they are going to do badly). This small practice is easy for children to do and remember, and it often creates distance from a thought. In this way, the thought doesn't have as much control over the child, so they react less to it and can choose what matters to them, even when the thought shows up, instead of having their mind boss them around and tell them what to do (and what not to do).

Choose What Matters

Choose what matters refers to values—things that a person cares about, that they are willing to work on. Values are different from goals, which are often temporary events with a final outcome (Twohig et al., 2008). For example, feeling connected to the soccer team is a value, whereas the team's winning the final game is a goal. In ACT, we encourage a child to choose what matters to them in various domains, such as family, school, and leisure, rather than choosing ones that they feel they ought to, or that are important to other people, such as parents, friends, and teachers.

Here is an example of a *choose what matters* exercise: Ask a child to imagine having an eleventh birthday party when they complete elementary school, and at the party their friends give a speech about them and say what they will remember about them when they go their separate ways to junior high school. Ask the child how they would like to be remembered by their classmates and where they currently see themself in terms of what matters to them. In other words, are they currently doing things that matter to them, and therefore are close to what matters to them, or are they not doing things that matter to them, and therefore far away? In ACT, the purpose of focusing on *choose what matters* is to help organize behavior in the direction of what is important for a person. Attaining specific goals is significant only to the extent that these achievements signal that the person is on course in terms of consistency with what matters to them.

Do What Matters

Do what matters refers to effective behaviors that tie in with the values identified in *choose what matters* (Hayes et al., 2006). In this aspect, ACT is very similar to traditional behavior therapy, which aims to change behaviors. Many behavior therapy methods can also be used as part of ACT, such as shaping (i.e., using reinforcement to gradually change behavior), goal setting, exposure (i.e., a technique in which a person is safely exposed to an anxiety-provoking stimulus, for example, going in an elevator), and skills acquisition (Hayes et al., 2006). In ACT, these methods are related to achieving goals, based on *choose what matters,* and to promoting ever-widening patterns of doing what matters. In contrast, in CBT, the aim of behavior-change methods is to maintain treatment goals, prevent relapses, and decrease psychological discomfort and functional impairment (Coyne et al., 2011).

Almost always, *do what matters* triggers both pleasant and unpleasant thoughts and feelings and usually includes psychological events that the child has previously avoided. For example, a child who is anxious that they might not perform well in the final basketball game of the season might choose to show up because they enjoy playing basketball, want to have fun with their friends, and don't want to let the team down by not attending.

Stay Here

When people dwell on memories, ruminate about why things occurred, and worry about the future, they are less present (Harris, 2009). The goal of *stay here* is being in direct contact with one's experiences, without trying to dismiss or minimize them (Coyne et al., 2011). In ACT, the outcome of *stay here* is more openness and flexibility in behavior (Coyne et al., 2011). An example of an exercise to develop this skill is mindful eating: noticing the smell, colors, taste, flavors, and texture of food and the sensation of the food in your mouth, and really staying here, catching yourself when you start to get caught up in your thoughts and are no longer focused on the food, then gently bringing your attention back to noticing the food.

Using the earlier example of the child who was concerned about their piano recital and was avoiding practicing in response to their anxious thoughts, we would encourage them to practice piano and stay here, really being aware of how the keys feel under their hands and fingers, attending to the sounds and volume of the music they are playing, noticing when their attention drifts away to thoughts of how they think they will perform in the recital, and bringing their attention back to the feel and sounds of playing the piano.

Note: Throughout the book, I will use the phrase "stay here" to refer to using the *stay here* process, even when the person I'm referring to isn't actually present. This is to maintain consistency and emphasize the language I use with children when teaching them this process.

Notice Yourself

Notice yourself can be defined as standing back and watching yourself. To help clients with this process, ACT uses mindfulness exercises, experiential exercises that build perspective taking, and metaphors (Hayes, Pistorello et al., 2012). Consider the example of a child who feels sad as it gets closer to the anniversary of their father's death: each time they feel sad at home, they go to their bedroom and lie on their bed, only leaving their bedroom to join their mother and siblings when they feel better. Sometimes they stay in their bedroom for hours because they feel sad, resulting in their missing out on eating dinner and playing board games with their family. You could help this child develop the skill of *notice yourself* by inviting them to participate in an experiential exercise where they imagine themself at home feeling sad and notice that they go to their bedroom and lie on their bed, where they often spend a lot of time, without leaving their bedroom until they feel less sad. Taking part in this exercise may help the child realize just how much time they are spending alone, waiting until they feel better to leave their room. As a result of doing this exercise with you in session, the child might start noticing themself at home when they're in their room feeling sad, and in response, they may join their family instead of staying in their room, even when they feel sad. This may help the child connect with their family and stay here, instead of being caught up in their thoughts.

Another experiential *notice yourself* exercise uses metaphor, where you could ask the child to imagine that they are standing on a beach, noticing their thoughts and feelings like waves that come to the shore—some strong and others gentle, none of which harm the shore.

The Goal of the ACT Kidflex: I Am Flexible

Although we talk about the processes of the ACT Kidflex (*let it be, let it go, choose what matters, do what matters, stay here,* and *notice yourself*) separately—addressing one or two at a time so that children can learn and experience them in a meaningful way—all of the processes combine to create *I am flexible* (stay here, notice what's happening without trying to change your thoughts and feelings, and keep going or change your actions when needed, to do what matters to you). Keep in mind that because *I am flexible* is the outcome of using the processes of the Kidflex, we don't directly teach it to the child.

At this point, you might be wondering whether children need to use all of the Kidflex processes in order to become flexible. They don't: they might use some of the processes in some situations, without needing to use them all. They might already be using a Kidflex process, so you might teach them how to use another process together with the one they're already using. For example, the child might struggle with *let it go,* which might result in their having great difficulty regulating their emotions. When they do not get their own way, they become very distressed, and shout and cry. But they are skilled in staying here, and often really immerse themself in activities and sports. You could encourage them to try letting their thoughts go when they become angry, and try to practice bringing their attention back to the present, noticing their surroundings, and engaging in what's happening around them, rather than being caught up in their thoughts of feeling very angry. This may help them regulate their emotions and stop shouting.

Now that we've finished looking at the ACT Kidflex, let's turn to a crucial aspect of conducting ACT known as the ACT stance.

The ACT Stance

Once I started using ACT with my own clients, not only did I notice obvious changes in terms of the actual therapeutic techniques I was using, but I also noticed that I was making several changes to *how* I interact with my clients. These changes have become key features of my therapeutic style and include the language I use with clients, the power dynamic between myself and my clients, my attention in sessions, my willingness to sometimes share my own difficulties, and practicing the therapeutic techniques in my own life. Making all of these changes—collectively referred to as the ACT stance—has had a very positive impact on my ability to quickly develop rapport with my clients, particularly children. Embracing the ACT stance will be vital for you as well in your work with children. Let's look now at each of these in greater detail.

Language

One of the changes I noticed that I made to my therapeutic stance after commencing my own journey learning ACT relates to language. During my undergraduate and postgraduate studies in psychology, and in clinical supervision as part of training to become a licensed psychologist, I trained in CBT, and my lecturers and supervisors referred to clients as "patients," consistent with a medical model. While I adopted this term for my own work, I noticed it didn't feel quite right for me. Out of curiosity, I researched the origin of the word "patient" and discovered that it originates from the Latin words "patiens" and "patior," which mean to suffer. This conveys the idea that those we help are unwell and need to be "fixed," or "cured" so they are no longer unwell, and will feel "better" as a result of treatment (Neuberger, 1999). The ACT stance differs markedly, and as such my own language has changed: I help "clients," rather than treating patients. (Note that I work in private practice and at a school, so this terminology is suitable for those settings, but you may work in settings such as hospitals where it is more appropriate to continue to refer to the people you work with as patients.)

One way that I apply language in sessions with children is by introducing myself by my first name. If the child or their parents refer to me as "Dr.," or "Dr. Black," or "Dr. Tamar," I ask that they please call me Tamar. My reason for doing this is that I want the child and their parent to see that I view myself as their equal. I also hope that if the child refers to me by my first name, they will be less intimated and feel more comfortable with the therapeutic process. (I understand, though, that in some organizations, such as schools, students are not permitted to refer to staff by their first name, while in others this may be optional. When I've worked in schools where I was given a choice of how students referred to me, I've elected for students to call me by my first name.)

Balance of Power

An equal balance of power between the ACT therapist and client is an important aspect of the ACT stance. There are several things that you can do to demonstrate this. As mentioned above, the language that you choose to use with your client, such as how you introduce yourself, gives the child and their parent a sense of whether you see the therapeutic relationship as equal.

Another way to demonstrate balance of power is by providing information and strategies to the child and their parent in a manner that invites their participation rather than from an authoritative stance. I do this by giving the child a choice of several exercises that we can do in sessions, instead of only one. If you have lots of experience in the problem or difficulty the child is seeing you for, you could inform the child and their parent that you've worked with lots of other children with the same problem or difficulty, and that you'd really like to try to help them. Introduce all exercises to the child as being completely optional: tell the child that it's up to them whether they choose to participate (we will look at voluntary participation in more detail in chapter 2).

HELPFUL HINT

When suggesting tasks for the child to do in between sessions to practice what they've learned, let the child know that they can do the exercise if they wish to, but that they don't have to.

At the beginning of the following session, ask the child if they were able to try to do the task that you suggested last session. I always preface this with something like "You may remember that last time we met, at the end of the session I suggested that when you are at home, you try the mindful breathing exercise to help you fall asleep. I'm wondering if you gave it a try. If you didn't, that's absolutely fine, I won't be disappointed or angry." If the child replies that they did try the home task, I ask if we could spend some time with them telling me how it went. I also usually add something like "Please don't feel that you have to tell me that it worked well if it wasn't helpful; please just tell me how it really went for you." This can demonstrate that you view the child as your equal and are open to hearing that your suggestions might not have been helpful. I find that telling children something like this helps to reassure them that they don't have to try to please me by saying that my suggestions were helpful.

Another way you can demonstrate that you view the balance of power as equal is to make sure you aren't spending most of the session talking, which is important when working with children. Too much talking by therapists is especially common for therapists new to ACT; in fact, it's something that I still watch for carefully in my own work. If you find yourself questioning whether you are talking too much about ACT in sessions with the child, ask yourself whether you are "talking about ACT rather than doing ACT" (Brock et al., 2015, p.140). This is often a helpful way to take a pause in the session and check in with yourself about what's happening.

HELPFUL HINT

If you notice that you have been talking to the child about ACT concepts rather than using interactive techniques, you can bring in an experiential exercise.

Stemming from this, it's also important to watch how much talking you are doing compared to the child so that you don't dominate the session, which might occur when you feel uncomfortable (Brock et al., 2015). This can also occur when you feel really excited about how the session is progressing, and you want to tell the child everything you can about ACT, perhaps to try to help them quickly. Too much talking on your part might also involve introducing far too many metaphors, which is likely to be confusing for the child. If you *do* want to use metaphors, I recommend using only one per session, making sure that it's developmentally appropriate for the child, using language they can understand (we will discuss language in more detail in chapters 3, 4, and 5 when we look at how to use the processes of the ACT Kidflex).

Stay Here in Sessions

The idea of staying here in sessions is echoed in *Mindfulness for Two* (Wilson, 2008), which features Wilson's beautiful suggestion that we see our clients as sunsets to be appreciated, instead of problems to be solved. Wilson suggests that our attention often gets caught up in the person's problems, which takes our attention, awareness, and appreciation away from the person in front of us.

I encourage you to try to stay here when you listen to your clients: really noticing them, taking in what they say, and appreciating them, rather than rushing to work out what's "wrong" with them. When you start to truly assume the *stay here* stance while listening to clients you have seen previously, your experience may feel akin to seeing them for the very first time, and you may in fact notice things and learn things not just about your clients, but also about your own reactions, that you haven't been aware of before.

Therapist Self-Disclosure

Many of the exercises used in ACT involve expressing difficult thoughts. Some ACT therapists use self-disclosure (although it is certainly not essential nor a requirement for effective and meaningful therapy, so if you don't feel comfortable using self-disclosure, or you don't wish to, you don't need to). To use self-disclosure effectively, you might let clients know (choosing appropriate examples) that you also have your own struggles, and, where appropriate, you may share a struggle of your own, including sharing the ACT techniques that you yourself have found helpful. I recommend sharing thoughts that are fairly neutral and common (for example, going to bed too late, or letting your room get messy). When using self-disclosure, it's important to take care not to do this in a didactic, lecturing way. Rather, this can be done by conveying your own vulnerability and normalizing your client's struggle, taking care not to undermine it.

Some of the children I work with feel anxious about returning to school after summer vacation, or after being absent from school for an extended period of time. Even though I have worked at the same school for nineteen years, I still feel nervous every year on the first day of school after summer vacation, so I might share this with children in order to let them know that what they're feeling is normal, and experienced by lots of people. I let the child know that I go to school even though I feel nervous, because my job really matters to me, and that feeling nervous can't actually harm me. This shows the child that I can feel nervous *and* still go to school, instead of letting feeling nervous stop me from going. I add that my nervousness shows up the most the night before the first day of school, or while I'm traveling to school, and when this happens, I notice how I feel, and I remind myself that there's probably several others at school who feel just like I do. Alternatively, when appropriate, if a child is anxious about presenting in front of the class, I share that I also get worried about speaking in front of big groups (especially at ACT conferences), and I let them know what matters to me about teaching people how to use ACT with children and adolescents, and that I would be missing out on lots of things if I gave into my fears and did not give a presentation.

Using self-disclosure can help show that you understand the child's experience, because you can relate to it yourself, which can help the child feel more comfortable discussing their thoughts and feelings with you. It's helpful to keep in mind that the child might feel there's something wrong with them because they worry about going to school, or giving presentations in front of the class, especially if no one has ever shared with them that they *also* have those experiences. Hearing this disclosure from you might bring great relief for the child and help reduce possible shame, embarrassment, or concerns about what you might think of them.

Self-disclosure is also appropriate when doing artwork alongside the child. When the therapy session involves an art exercise (examples for art exercises are provided in chapters 3, 4 and 5), I also participate, making sure that my artwork is very simple (I purposely draw stick figures so that it looks like it has been done by a child), to reduce the possibility of the child feeling intimidated or uncomfortable about theirs. You can invite the child to share their artwork first, and then share yours.

The more you as therapist model *your own use* of ACT techniques, instead of just suggesting them, the better. The child will actually hear that you *also* have difficulties (appropriate for sharing with the child), which don't stop you from doing things. This will also demonstrate your use of the same techniques that you are recommending to them, which will likely have a positive impact on the child's buy-in (and increase their view that you actually *do* know what you are talking about).

HELPFUL HINT

The child might have seen several other therapists before seeing you, but you might be the first to share strategies that you have found helpful for yourself. This might score you big points with the child for credibility, help them feel more comfortable with the therapeutic process, and also help you build rapport.

Sometimes it's hard to know as the therapist whether it's appropriate to engage in self-disclosure with the child. It's a good idea to ask yourself what the purpose of disclosing your own struggle is. You might also try thinking of a colleague whom you respect greatly and ask yourself what their reaction would be if you told them you were uncertain whether to disclose this struggle to your client. Or you could imagine that you were to contact the leading professional association in your field and ask their opinion; what would they be likely to advise you? Another way of considering this dilemma is to ask yourself, if the door to your office were open and other staff walked past your office and heard you disclosing your own difficulties to the child, would the staff think this was appropriate?

Try the Techniques Yourself

If you are going to use ACT with any clients, regardless of their age, it's also important that you have a go at using the techniques in your own life, so that you make suggestions that you know are actually effective. If the child then says something like "These ideas sound strange or weird," and you have tried the techniques yourself, you could share with them that you had the exact same thought when you first learned these techniques, but you tried them anyway and found that they were helpful for you. Sometimes I preempt this by letting the child know that the strategies I am about to suggest might sound a little strange, and that I actually thought they were a bit strange when I first learned them myself!

When addressing *let it be*, for example, I often recommend to the child that they say hello to their thoughts and tell their thoughts how great it is to see them (Twohig, 2014), saying something like "Hi worries, it's really great to see you, you are looking fabulous today!" Then I ask the child what they think of this suggestion, and whether it sounds strange, or weird. Most children smile or laugh in response and agree that the technique is a bit strange or weird, and I reply that I had the same thought when I first heard it. I find that acknowledging this also helps me build rapport with the child.

HELPFUL HINT

After you have read this book, have a go at using ACT in your own life first to see how it feels and what happens, being open to whatever shows up.

Tread the ACT Waters Slowly

Depending on your familiarity with ACT, you might find yourself in any of these situations:

- Even if you have already done an introductory and perhaps an advanced ACT training workshop that focused on using ACT with adults, you might not know how to apply what you've learned to using ACT with children (this was certainly the case for me when I first began learning about ACT).

- If you are an experienced therapist who usually works with children, you may feel that ACT is similar to how you already work with this population.
- Whether you work with children or adults, if this is the first ACT book you are reading, the concepts in ACT may feel familiar and consistent with what matters to you.
- ACT may seem *really* different, unfamiliar, and counterintuitive to what you learned in your studies and training, and perhaps how you've been working with children.

Whatever your particular situation is, take this journey slowly, and notice if you start to put pressure on yourself to understand it all straight away. If ACT seems hard, and your mind tells you that you will never be able to understand it, and you feel discouraged, I encourage you to sit with these thoughts and feelings, thanking your mind for them, without giving up on learning how to use ACT.

When I first learned about ACT, I was very uncertain of how and where to start using it with my clients. And now when I learn new ACT techniques, I am still always nervous the first time I try the techniques with a client. What I've found really helpful is to let the child know that

I've just learned something new and haven't tried the exercise with anyone yet. I tell them that I don't know if I'm going to follow the instructions correctly, or whether the exercise is going to be helpful for them. In my experience, children are usually quite excited to be the first to try a new therapeutic exercise, and they're usually very understanding (and forgiving) if I make mistakes.

HELPFUL HINT

Start trying out what you read in this book with clients, even if your mind tells you that you aren't ready. The more you practice using ACT, the more proficient you will become in its use.

I have tried to write this book as the book that I wished was available when I first learned about ACT, in the hope that it will encourage you to use ACT with children. When I attended my first ACT training workshop, a two-day workshop with Russ Harris in October 2007, Russ began the workshop by encouraging us to learn from as many different ACT trainers as possible. Following this, when I began clinical supervision in ACT the following year, the most significant thing my supervisor said to me was that ACT looks really different from one therapist to another. Having attended workshops with several leading ACT experts and having read many ACT books, I have come to fully understand and appreciate both of these insights.

My own style of ACT is quite eclectic in that I have borrowed some bits and pieces from several different ACT experts, and I've adapted the strategies and exercises to make them simpler in language and application, to be developmentally appropriate for children. I have also made up many of my own. I encourage you to do the same with this book: read it with an open and willing mind, and by all means, feel free to adapt exercises as you to wish to, making sure to use simple language that children can understand. You can also have a go at creating your own exercises.

Conclusion

In this chapter, you have learned about ACT, how it differs from CBT, and why it's suitable for use with children. You have been introduced to the ACT Kidflex and its six processes (*let it be, let it go, choose what matters, do what matters, stay here,* and *notice yourself*), and you've learned the various aspects of the ACT stance. The next chapter focuses on the first session with children and their parents, including introducing yourself to children and using an ACT case conceptualization template to obtain a history of the presenting problem or difficulty through an ACT lens.

CHAPTER 2

The First Session and ACT Case Conceptualization

Now that you have an understanding of ACT and how it can be modified for working with children, we will look at how to conduct the first session with the child (and their parent or caregiver where appropriate). This includes looking at what to watch out and listen for. I will also take you through a case conceptualization template developed especially for use with children aged five to twelve years, showing you how to use it, including what questions to ask children and their parents. Finally, we'll look at how to introduce ACT to children and how to respond when children are resistant to engaging in therapy.

Who's in the Therapy Room?

Unless I know in advance of a reason that the parent's presence in the session might be inappropriate, or unhelpful, I ask both the child and parent to attend the first session together, at least for the history-taking part at the beginning. This way, we are all clear about what information I am receiving, and I obtain pertinent information before therapy begins. Otherwise, if I only see the child, and the parent remains in the waiting area, at the end of the consultation the parent may ask the child, "Did you remember to tell Tamar about _____?" and the child may reply that they forgot. It's often something that's important that would have been helpful for me to know during the session, rather than only finding out about after the session ended.

After asking the parent to join the child and me, I add that if the child would prefer that their parent not stay in the room with us for the whole session, that's okay; their parent can leave after they've told me about why they want the child to see me. In some cases I may already have met with the parent prior to seeing the child. Even when that has occurred, I still like the parent to briefly explain their reasons for bringing their child to see me, so that the child knows why they are there. Also, it sometimes also helps the child to feel more comfortable and willing to contribute to the discussion if their parent talks first. I then give the child an opportunity to respond by asking, "How much of what mom/dad just said do you agree with?" or "Do you feel that mom/dad got that correct?" Sometimes partway through the first session, the child instructs the parent, "You can leave now," and I go with that, allowing the child to direct who is in the room, and I suggest that the parent sit in the waiting area (which most parents are happy to do).

Sometimes the child will want to talk to me about things that their parent might not be aware of, or they might not wish to burden or upset their parent by disclosing issues (or the severity) in front of their parent. The relationship with the parent, or something that the parent has done, may also be the cause or source of the child's distress, so it's important to allow the child the space to talk to you on their own if they ask to, as there may be issues involving their safety they wish to discuss. Honoring the child's request to talk to them alone will likely make the child feel that you have heard and listened to them, and that you respect them, which I find also assists with building rapport.

Now that we've discussed who's in the therapy room, it might be helpful to consider how to introduce yourself, particularly if you haven't done therapy with children before.

Introducing Yourself and Outlining the Structure of the Session

I start the first session by saying something similar to the following:

My name is Tamar, and I am a psychologist: that's a pretty big word for someone who talks to people and tries to help them. Some of the children I work with call me a "talking doctor," and I think that's a really good description. What I do here in this office is see children, teenagers, and parents, who might come to see me because there are things that are making them worried, or sad, or angry, or frightened, or they might be having difficulties working out ways to deal with things. Sometimes there might be things happening at home to cause how they are feeling, or at school, which might have to do with learning, or things happening with friends, or other children, or teachers. I listen, then I come up with ideas for how children might be able to do things a bit differently, so they feel that they can cope or manage things better. How does that sound? Do you have any questions that you would like to ask me?

I give a short explanation of confidentiality, and what that means, with specific examples of when I would not be able to keep what the child says confidential ("between you and me"). I also explain why, and add examples of who I would need to tell (for example, their parents or caregiver, and sometimes their referring doctor), and I explain that if that does need to occur, I will try to let the child know before I speak to anyone about them. I also tell the child that where possible, I will try to give them the option of being present when I have those discussions. I also inform them that I will not be talking to any of their friends, and that I will not speak to their teachers about them unless they give me permission to.

After introducing myself, it's time to explain to the child what's going to happen today, in the first session. I say something similar to the following:

> Today I would really like to hear from you what life is like for you. (*I try to avoid using the phrase "What it's like to be in your shoes" because it might be confusing for the child, especially if they are neurodiverse, such as autistic children, or have language difficulties, and may perceive this phrase literally and think that I am going to want to wear their shoes, which may make them feel uncomfortable or worried.*)
>
> While I would like to hear from you today (*direct this to the child rather than their parent*), sometimes children are shy or uncomfortable meeting someone new and talking about their difficulties straight away, so if you would like your parent to start and let me know why they have brought you to see me, that is absolutely fine!
>
> If there's anything that your parent says and you think to yourself, *No, that's not right*, or *That's not how it is*, or *That's wrong*, I want you to tell us that you disagree, and tell me how things are for you. This is because you are *the* most important person in this room, and what you feel and think

are really important to me *(the child usually looks pleased to hear this, and letting them know that you want to hear their opinions can be a good way to start to build rapport with them).*

If you decide you *don't* want to do any of the talking in here today, and prefer to leave it for mom/dad/caregiver to talk, that's absolutely okay too. I hope that once you get to know me, you might feel willing and more comfortable to talk to me about how you are feeling, but I understand that you might not be ready today, and that's okay *(this also models my own use of let it be).*

Sometimes children will have already tried therapy with another therapist (or several) before seeing you. When you know this has occurred, it's helpful to hear from the child what strategies they can recall that their therapist suggested. In my own work, I find that even if the child or their parent doesn't know the name of the therapy used, asking if they can recall some of the strategies will often give me clues about which therapy has been used. If the child and/or parent can't recall any particular strategies from the previous therapist, that's important data too! Ask the parent whether they were present during their child's sessions, and if not, whether they received feedback about what occurred in sessions and their child's progress, and whether they were given strategies to use at home with their child in between sessions in order to remind the child and reinforce what was done in sessions.

After receiving this information, at the end of the session you can inform the child and their parent about how you work, including the importance of providing the parent with feedback about the strategies you use in sessions as well as giving the parent examples of how they can help the child to practice these at home. It's important to gauge the parent's response to this, which will often give you an indication of the parent's level of interest in and capacity for being actively involved in their child's therapeutic journey.

HELPFUL HINT

Tell the parent who brings the child to sessions that you would like to work collaboratively with them to support their child, as this often leads to greater and quicker treatment gains.

At this point in the session, my own practice is to explain that even if the child chooses for their parent *not* to attend the sessions, I would still like to give the parent feedback for about ten minutes at the end of sessions—not about the specific details of what the child has said, but about the strategies I have taught the child. That way, the parent and I work together as a team to support the child, and I also get to teach the parent about ACT, rather than only teaching the child. I find that teaching the parent some new techniques is usually helpful not only for the child, but also for the parent who is often trying hard to provide support to their child.

Sometimes the parent will then turn to their child and comment, "I might learn to do things differently, which might be good, or helpful; I am open to changing the way I do things." This response shows acceptance, openness, and willingness (let it be) by the parent, and also shows the child that the parent is already valuing the therapeutic process, which might have a positive impact on the child, especially if their relationship with their parent is conflictual. As it is often the parent who initiates therapy on behalf of their child, rather than the child themself, the child may become more motivated and willing to attend therapy if they see that their parent is open to receiving guidance about changing their own behavior, instead of the whole focus being the behavior of the child.

Wearing an Imaginary Pair of ACT Lenses

In the therapy room with children, I imagine that I am wearing a pair of ACT lenses to watch and listen carefully for important information that helps me develop my case conceptualization (covered in detail later in this chapter). This includes watching and listening for what coping strategies the child is currently using, what isn't working for them, and what strategies they may have used in the past. If the parent is present, I also watch the relationship between the child and parent, including the manner in which they speak to and react to each other. Carefully watching and listening will help you to develop insight into where therapy needs to begin using the ACT Kidflex. In this section, I'll cover specific ways that wearing your ACT lenses can help prepare you for conceptualizing the case and working with the child and their parent in therapy.

Watching for Avoidance. When the discussion between you and the child strikes a nerve for the child, or focuses on something that the child cares deeply about, you might observe avoidant behavior in the child. In this instance, you may notice the child do things that are indicative of how they cope with discomfort in their day-to-day life. For example, if the child talks about a situation where they felt sad or worried, and you ask them to try to recall specific thoughts that their mind came up with at that time, or you ask when feeling sad or worried usually shows up, or where they feel sad or worried in their body, you might notice that the child shows signs of avoidance, such as changing the topic or pulling out a toy or cell phone.

Listening for Rules and Being Right. A child may be fixated on rules and being right, and might argue when you suggest alternatives to how they do things. Children who do this can also be very good at giving you lots and lots of reasons why they can't do certain things, and they may hold on to their beliefs quite tightly. To detect this, you might listen for statements such as "I don't go to parties; parties are noisy." In ACT, this is known as *fusion*. You can consider this data in your thinking about how to increase the child's *psychological flexibility* (see chapter 1 for more detail), perhaps by setting up tasks focusing on *let it be* and *let it go* (both in sessions and in their daily life) as well as *do what matters*.

Listening for Choosing What Matters. Some of the things I carefully listen for include any statements about choosing what matters to the child, and whether what matters to the child and parent are congruent. For example, the child might wish to develop greater independence and take the public bus home from school with their friends, instead of having their parent pick them up. The child has never taken the bus before and tells their parent that although they would like to start, they feel anxious about doing so. You could ask the parent how they feel about the child's taking the bus home. The parent might reply that the child is too young to take the bus and that the child's anxiety is validation that they aren't ready to take the bus. As a result, the parent insists on continuing to pick up the child from school. In this case, what matters to the child and their parent are *not* congruent.

I also listen for any mention of whether the child is avoiding particular situations, places, or people, or whether they have stopped going somewhere or stopped doing something that they previously enjoyed because of the presenting problem or difficulty. For example, you might discover that a client of yours loves playing soccer, but after they did not perform well in the last soccer match, they stopped attending training for fear of feeling embarrassed in front of their teammates.

Listening for Doing What Matters. We also want to listen carefully for any mention of something that the child might have done in the past that mattered to them, even though they were sad, scared, worried, or the like. In particular, consider this in terms of the specific problem or difficulty the child is seeing you for. You can ascertain this by asking the child if they have ever done anything that mattered to them even though they felt sad/scared/worried. For example, if the child is seeing you for anxiety, ask, "Have you ever done anything that you were really worried about doing, but you did it anyway, such as performing in a play, recital, or concert, or presenting in front of the class?" The child might reply that they attend drama classes and performed in a play as the main character, even though they felt really nervous in front of the large audience.

In the case conceptualization template in the next section, you will see how you can ask the child about something they might have done in the past that mattered to them. This is one of the most important pieces of data you can gather, as it will give you information about whether they have been willing to experience discomfort in the past and still do something that matters to them. This can underpin your work with the child and give you something to remind them of, which can motivate and encourage them to do the actions that matter to them (*do what matters*) even if they experience discomfort, because there's something important about doing it that matters to them (*choose what matters*).

Listening Carefully to the Parent Too. It's also important to listen for the strategies that the parent might be giving their child and to note to yourself whether these are consistent with the ACT approach. For example, the parent might be encouraging their child to try attending a sleepover party at their best friend's home even though the child is worried that they might feel scared. This response is consistent with the ACT approach. Alternatively, if the parent recommends to their child that they *don't* attend the sleepover, in an effort to shield or prevent them from experiencing discomfort, the parent is promoting the use of avoidant behavior, which is not consistent with the aim of ACT—psychological flexibility.

Developing an ACT Case Conceptualization

If you have already used ACT with adolescents or adults, you might be familiar with developing a case conceptualization. This usually involves using an ACT case conceptualization template, generally as part of the first session with the child, to obtain a history of the presenting problem or difficulty. Then, you'll want to ask any other questions you might have that weren't covered by the template. You might also conduct a clinical interview for diagnostic purposes, if relevant. Sometimes, when the child (and possibly their parent) has reported a lengthy history, there might not be sufficient time to start a clinical interview in the first session, so you can do so at the beginning of the second session.

HELPFUL HINT

Feel free to download the case conceptualization template from the book's website (see the end of the book for more information) and have the template in front of you in your first session with the child.

Where appropriate, I find it helpful to develop a case conceptualization from the perspective of both the child and their parent (which in some cases may be different). I find this particularly beneficial when working with younger children, as it helps me identify differences in coping strategies between the child and their parent, as well as the specific areas in which I will need to provide strategies to the child's parents.

I developed the following template specifically for use with children aged five to twelve years; you can also use it when working with parents or caregivers in regard to their child. Please go to http://www.newharbinger.com/49760, where you can download a version of this template with room for you to write the child and parent's responses.

ACT Case Conceptualization Template For Children

This is designed to be used as part of taking the child's history. You can ask the child the questions directly, or ask the child's parent(s) or caregivers the questions regarding their child.

1. What is the main problem or difficulty you are having?

(When working with parents: what do you think is the main problem or difficulty your child is having?)

.

2. When did this start?

.

3. What do you do when this problem or difficulty shows up or happens?

If the parent is present, you can also ask:

What do you do in response to your child feeling this way?

If the parent isn't present, you can ask the child:

What does your parent do when you feel like this? Do both your parents respond in the same way?

4. Where does the behavior usually occur, and what happens right *before* the behavior occurs?

5. What happens right *after* the behavior occurs?

6. Is this the first time this has been a problem or difficulty for you?

(If the child is unsure or unable to recall, and their parent is present, you can ask the parent this question in relation to the child.)

If it isn't, can you remember what you did to try to make things better for yourself previously, or last time?

7. Are you avoiding doing anything, or seeing anyone, or going anywhere because of this problem or difficulty?

If the child answers yes, you can also ask:

Can you think of another time when your mind told you not to do something, because you were_____ (sad/afraid/worried/etc.), but you did it anyway?

.

8. Is there anything you are missing out on because of how you try to manage this problem or difficulty?

9. Do you spend a lot of time thinking about this problem or difficulty, and if you do, about how much time per day do you spend thinking about it, or doing things to avoid it?

.

10. Do you ever notice yourself thinking about your problem or difficulty, or doing things to avoid it? And do you have any difficulties concentrating on what's happening around you, for example, in class, or at home, because you're thinking about your problem or difficulty?

.

11. Do you think what you have been doing to manage this problem or difficulty is helping you?

If the child says yes, you can ask:

Does what you are doing create or cause any more problems or difficulties for you?

Or: Is there something you are doing that isn't helping you?

.

12. Is what you have been doing *working* for you?

13. Let's pretend that I had a magic wand; I wish I did, but I don't, as magic wands aren't real, but let's just pretend that I do. Imagine it could help you cope with your thoughts and feelings, and you could start doing things that *really* matter to you, or you could do these things more often. Perhaps feeling _____ (sad/afraid/worried/etc.) has stopped you from doing this, or stopped you from doing it often. If you could start doing this thing, or you could do it more often, what would you be doing?

Next, we'll go through the case conceptualization template in greater detail and discuss how to use it. I'll provide suggestions on how to ask each question, including alternative ways of asking questions, in case the child isn't sure what you are asking about. Note that for all questions directed to or about parents, you can replace the word "parent" with "caregiver" if the child lives with a caregiver.

Notes on Using the Case Conceptualization Template

1. **What is the main problem or difficulty you are having?**

    If the child is unable to answer this first question, or is very young (for example, five to eight years old), you can make this question more specific by asking any of these questions:

    • "Do you know why your mom/dad/caregiver/doctor/teacher thought that it might be a good idea for you to see me?"

    • "Is there something happening for you that you would like some help with?"

    • "What does your mom/dad/caregiver/doctor/teacher think that I might be able to help you with?"

2. **When did this start?**

    Children may be unable to recall when the problem or difficulty arose, especially is it's been happening for a long time, or if they are very young. If this is the case, you might ask, "Can you remember the last time this *wasn't* a problem or difficulty for you?"

    To obtain more information, you might ask the child or their parent about specific behaviors that the child engages in. For example, if the child has been diagnosed with social anxiety disorder or separation anxiety disorder, or if there's no previous diagnosis that you are aware of but you already know that the child becomes highly anxious in social situations, you could ask, "When was the last time you walked into school on your own without your parent, or slept at a friend's home, or attended a party without your parent?"

3. **What do you do when this problem or difficulty shows up or happens?**

Another way to ask this would be "What might we see you do when this is happening?" If the child isn't sure how the problem or difficulty impacts their behavior, I say, "Let's pretend that I was to give you a video camera, and you carry it with you for about one day and night. I'm *not* going to do this, but let's just pretend that I did, and that it would record everything you do, then you would bring it back here and we would watch it together. When this problem or difficulty shows up or happens, what would we see you do?" If the child is able to describe what happens, you can then ask, "What happens after that?" (adapted from Harris, 2009).

If the child is unsure, the following example might provide clarification: "If the problem or difficulty is that you feel sad, you might go to your bedroom whenever you feel sad at home, or you might leave school early and go home when you feel sad. You might stay in your bedroom until you don't feel so sad anymore, which might be a long time, like a few hours. I'm not suggesting that you do that; I want to give you an example of how a person's feelings can make them feel that they need to do something or go somewhere until they feel better. Does this ever happen to you?" I do this to start to introduce the *notice yourself* process, and I encourage the child to start to observe their own behavior and how it impacts them.

This part of the ACT case conceptualization also involves finding out what the parent does in relation to the child's problem or difficulty; whether they always respond in the same way; and, if there is more than one parent, whether both respond in the same way.

If a parent is present, ask the parent:

What do you do in response to your child feeling this way?

If a parent is not present, ask the child:

What does your parent do when you feel like this? Do both your parents respond in the same way?

Once you have this information, you can start to think about (without asking the child) whether one of the parents might actually be reinforcing the behavior—meaning that the parent's response increases the likelihood of the child engaging in the same behavior again in the future. Also bear in mind that parents can respond differently to their child's behavior, which is especially common when parents don't live in the same home. When this occurs, the child might be confused by the different responses of their parents, and as a result, be unsure of how to cope with the problem or difficulty.

4. **Where does the behavior usually occur, and what happens right before the behavior occurs?**

The purpose of this question is to gauge whether the behavior occurs only in one environment (such as school or home). Ask the child who is with them when the behavior occurs (perhaps a parent or family member, or someone at school) and what happens right before that might lead to them engaging in this behavior (i.e., triggering this behavior). This will help you identify the environment where the child might need to use ACT strategies most. If the behavior occurs at school, you might need to ask for the child's and parent's consent to provide some recommendations to the child's teacher, or you can provide recommendations to the parent to forward to the teacher. If the behavior occurs only at home, you can provide recommendations to the parent about strategies they can use at home in order to support the child.

5. **What happens right *after* the behavior occurs?**

It's important that you try to find out from the child whether there's something that happens right after they engage in the particular behavior, which may also tell you whether someone or something is reinforcing the behavior. If the child isn't sure, you could ask them how other people react when they do this behavior. For example, if a child tells their teacher when they are feeling anxious at school and asks for permission to go home, ask how the teacher reacts. The child might inform you that the teacher always calls their parent to pick them up from school when they ask to go home, instead of having the child stay at school for the rest of the day. You can then ask the child how they feel about going home from school early. The child may reply that they feel better when they leave school because they are no longer anxious. These responses from the teacher and parent may be positively reinforcing the child's avoidant behavior, thereby making it more likely that the child will ask their teacher for permission to go home the next time they feel anxious.

6. **Is this the first time this has been a problem or difficulty for you? If it isn't, can you remember what you did to try to make things better for you previously, or last time?**

   If you find out from the child that they have experienced this same problem or difficulty in the past (for example, feeling sad), you can then ask them if they are able to remember how they coped previously or last time, and whether these strategies were helpful. This will tell you whether the child's previous coping strategies are consistent with those used in ACT, and if they are, you might be able to incorporate some of the child's previous strategies into your work with them. If the strategies the child previously used are *not* consistent with ACT, you might wish to explain to the child (and their parent if appropriate) after completing the case conceptualization process how ACT differs from the strategies the child used previously. If the child is unable to answer this question, or does not wish to, you could ask their parent the question in relation to the child. If you can't obtain information about this question, that's okay.

7. **Are you avoiding doing anything, or seeing anyone, or going anywhere because of this problem or difficulty?**

When the child has stopped doing things that matter to them, or is avoiding doing things or going to places (for example, school, summer camps, parties, grandparents' house, friends' houses, etc.), I also ask:

Can you think of another time when your mind told you *not* to do something, because you were _____ (sad/afraid/worried/etc.), but you did it anyway?

HELPFUL HINT

Use the word that the child has used to describe their problem or difficulty. I do not usually use the terms "depressed" or "anxious" with children of this age group as they might not know what it means, and I don't want to label the child with something they may not have been diagnosed with *even* if they or their parent uses that term. If the child has not been diagnosed (or perhaps has not been diagnosed correctly), you may need to also assess the child for disorders such as major depressive disorder and/or an anxiety disorder, which may include providing questionnaires to the child (depending on their age) and their parent and teacher.

You may have noticed in the above question that I have started to introduce the phrase "when your mind told you," which is a *let it go* technique we'll look at in detail in chapter 3. By using ACT-consistent language in the history-taking session, I am starting to introduce the child to ACT and beginning to show them (and their parent, if present) what therapy using ACT looks like. This is helpful for the child (and parent) when deciding whether to engage in therapy with me.

When I ask children if they can recall another time when their mind told them not to do something, I find that providing examples of what the child might have done previously helps the child to understand what I am asking about (for example, performing in a school play/end of year concert/musical, giving a presentation in front of the class, going on a big slide at a park or water park, or playing on a sports team). Sometimes it's difficult for the child to think of something, so if the parent is present, I ask the parent if they can recall something their child did despite being sad/afraid/worried. Usually, parents can think of something fairly bold pretty quickly, which the child can also recall. The parent often shows visible pride and delight in describing this activity, which may be encouraging and affirming for the child. If the parent is not present, and the child is unable to recall any examples, you can let them know that's okay, and that they can let you know if they think of any examples later.

8. **Is there anything you are missing out on because of how you try to manage this problem or difficulty?**

In my opinion, one of the most important parts of case conceptualization is finding out from the child what they think they are missing out on due to *how* they try to manage the problem or difficulty. If the child clearly articulates what matters to them, especially in the first session, and can identify what they might be missing out on because of their coping strategy or strategies, it's a very good sign that they are likely to respond well to ACT. I also find that asking this question helps me to obtain buy-in from the child for ACT, because if the child *does* feel that they are missing out on something, they will often be motivated to engage in therapy and learn some other coping strategies.

After asking this question, you can also ask the child, "If this *wasn't* a problem or difficulty for you, what would you be doing that you are not doing now?" If the child is able to answer this, you can then ask, "What is it about that that matters to you?" When discussing what matters to children about particular situations, places, or events, I recommend that you describe what matters as "the things that are important to you." My own practice is to then repeat the behavior the child articulated. For example, if the child said that they want to be able to walk into school without their parent but are too afraid to, I would say, "Walking into school without your parent is the stuff that's going to be a big part of our work together." I find that doing this helps to make it clear for the child what our sessions will focus on, which can also help increase the child's buy-in and motivation and reduce concerns or anxiety about attending therapy.

You can also let the child know that if they return to see you, your goal will be to try to help them do the things they feel like they aren't able to do, or feel like they can't do at the moment. You might have noticed that I haven't mentioned anything about trying to change the child's thoughts so that they won't *feel* afraid, or helping them to feel *better*. This is because in ACT, we don't try to change a person's thoughts or feelings, or try to do anything to make a person feel better. Instead, when using ACT, our aim is to help the child accept their thoughts and feelings (*let it be*) and reduce their use of avoidance as a coping strategy, even if difficult thoughts and feelings show up, such as anxiety about walking into school without their parent.

9. **Do you spend a lot of time thinking about this problem or difficulty, and if you do, about how much time per day do you spend thinking about it, or doing things to avoid it?**

This may be the first time that the child has considered how much time they spend thinking about their problem or difficulty. Doing so may help them realize that they do spend a lot of time thinking about it (even if they don't know exactly *how* much time) or doing things to avoid it. Asking this question can also help the child be more receptive to receiving assistance, especially if their problem or difficulty takes up a lot of their time each day.

10. **Do you ever notice yourself thinking about your problem or difficulty, or doing things to avoid it? And do you have any difficulties concentrating on what's happening around you, for example, in class, or at home, because you're thinking about your problem or difficulty?**

Asking the child this question will give you insight into whether the child is aware of when they are thinking about their problem or difficulty or engaging in behaviors to try to avoid it. It will also give you information about whether the child is distracted by their thoughts and feelings, or whether they are able to stay in the present and focus on what's happening around them. If the child *does* tell you that it's hard to concentrate because of the problem or difficulty, ask where it is hardest to concentrate, such as at home or at school. This may help you and the child identify what or who might trigger the problem or difficulty, or make it worse.

11. **Do you think what you have been doing to manage this problem or difficulty is helping you?**

   If the child says yes, you can ask:

   Does what you are doing create or cause any more problems or difficulties for you?

   Or:

   Is there something you are doing that isn't helping you?

   When you ask the child this question, you might need to explain what you are referring to by "helping you." For example, if the child is anxious about attending parties and doesn't attend parties whenever they feel anxious, ask, "Does staying home instead of going to parties help you?" If the child says yes, ask, "Is there something you do when you feel anxious about going to a party that *doesn't* help you?" The child might reply that staying home does help, because then they don't feel anxious. If this occurs, I don't recommend trying to convince the child that what they do in order to not feel anxious might create even more problems or difficulties, because the child is likely to become defensive. Instead, I find that offering a hypothetical example about another child can be more helpful, because when the focus is shifted to someone else, the child might be able to be more objective and consider the issue from another perspective.

You could give the child an example to illustrate this, like the following: "Let's think about a child who stays home instead of going to school because they are worried about not playing well in the basketball game, and as a result of their not attending, the team won't have enough players to participate in the basketball competition. The child spends the whole day feeling sad and guilty about letting their team down, and thinking about how if they had gone to school, the team might have played well and they might be celebrating with them by having a pizza party after school. Avoiding doing something might help prevent the child from feeling sad or being worried, but it might not be helpful, because they might end up missing out on things."

Then, you can come back to the reason the child is seeing you, and ask whether they might miss out on anything when they don't go to parties. The child might reply that they feel bad for letting the friend down who had the party, or that when they go to school on a Monday after missing a party on the weekend, the other children talk about the party at recess, and they feel sad or left out. When you ask the child about whether they think that what they are doing is actually helping, you may also receive some really useful information from the child about what they've already tried, what strategies their parents have suggested, and what strategies they think are unhelpful, or haven't worked for them.

Based on the child's and possibly their parent's responses to question 11, there are some important considerations for you to make at this point. First, are the strategies being used by the child (and their parent) *short-term solutions* that may promote avoidance, or are they *long-term strategies* that are likely to be helpful not only immediately, but also in the future? We can think of short-term solutions as attempts to reduce the child's immediate distress (using the above example, allowing the child to stay home from school when they are worried about the basketball game). By contrast, a long-term strategy is designed to help the child in the present and future, and doesn't create or cause any more problems or difficulties for the child (for example, the parent sends the child to school even when they're worried about the basketball game, and asks the teacher to check in with the child during the day and provide encouragement about the game).

If the parent allows the child to stay home whenever they are worried, the parent promotes the use of avoidance, which is *not* going to be a helpful strategy in the long run. When the child does attend school, their worries usually settle once the school day begins, and they have fun with their friends at recess and lunch. However, the parent might not consider this when they allow the child to stay home. While allowing the child to stay home may prevent the child from feeling worried, it may promote the use of avoidant and rigid behavior.

HELPFUL HINT

At this point in developing your case conceptualization, try to consider the *function* (purpose) of the child's behavior and also the function of their parent's behavior.

It's quite possible that the behavior the parent is encouraging results in taking the child away from what matters to them, rather than toward what matters. This can occur without the parent intending to do so, in their efforts to rescue and protect their child from difficult thoughts and feelings. In some cases, this might be driven by the parent's own fears that experiencing particular thoughts, feelings, memories, physical sensations, urges, or behaviors will be harmful for the child (especially if the parent has their own history of mental health struggles).

12. **Is what you have been doing *working* for you?**

This question is somewhat similar to the second part of question 11, but with a slight distinction. You might need to explain to the child that now that you have heard about what does and what doesn't help them, you would like to know whether what they have been doing might actually make things *worse* for them—in other words, do they feel worse or do things become worse because of what they do to try to manage the problem or difficulty? Asking this question will give you great insight into how willing the child might be to receive new ideas and try out some new techniques to manage their problem or difficulty. If the child expresses clearly that nothing they have tried works, that might also be an indication that they will be very receptive to trying ACT and be quite motivated to participate in sessions.

When the child lets me know that the strategies they have tried aren't working for them, I often inform them that the ideas they will hear from me are likely to be very different, and often quite the opposite, of what they have already tried. The child may also tell me what their parent has recommended they do, whether they have tried their parent's suggestions, and if so, whether the suggestions worked for them.

If the child tells me about strategies they have tried that are not consistent with ACT (for example, the child may say that their parent told them to think of happy thoughts before going to sleep, or not to think about things that worry them), and adds that the strategies don't work or aren't helpful, I will say something like "Trying to tell our minds what to think, or what *not* to think, is really hard, and I also find it really hard to do this." The reason that I do this is to start to gently introduce the child to ACT. I also make a note for myself that when I provide feedback to the child's parent (where appropriate), I will need to include examples of strategies that aren't consistent with ACT, so I can make it very clear to the parent which strategies I recommend and which strategies I don't recommend. I also make sure to include a gentle explanation of *why* I am recommending particular strategies, so as not to offend the parent or make them feel that they are being criticized.

13. **Let's pretend that I had a magic wand; I wish I did, but I don't, as magic wands aren't real, but let's just pretend that I do. Imagine it could help you cope with your thoughts and feelings, and you could start doing things that *really* matter to you, or you could do these things more often. Perhaps feeling _____ (sad/afraid/worried/etc.) has stopped you from doing this, or stopped you from doing it often. If you could start doing this thing, or you could do it more often, what would you be doing?**

This question, which I adapted from De Shazer (1988), is my favorite part of case conceptualization as it allows me to obtain information from the child about really what matters to them. If the child doesn't know how to answer, you could ask the following:

• "If I could help you, and things were to improve for you, what might be different?"

• "If you and I were to see each other a few times, and then after that you felt that I had helped you, and things improved for you, what is something that you might start to do, or do more of, that you feel like you can't or aren't able to do now?"

You might have noticed that I used the word "improved" rather than "feeling better." The reason for this is that when we use ACT, we don't promote feeling "better"; rather, we try to help our clients start doing the things that matter to them, without allowing how they feel to stop them from doing these things.

If, after asking the questions above, the child *still* isn't sure what you are talking about, it might be helpful to give them some examples, such as:

• putting up their hand in class and answering a question, even when they are worried that their answer might be incorrect

• going to a party, even if they are worried that they won't know everyone there or might not have a good time

• going on vacation with their family, even though they can remember that they didn't have a great time on vacation last year

• trying out for the school play, even though they feel that they aren't good at acting

I find that when I give children specific examples like the ones above, they are usually able to understand what I am referring to and can come up with something they wish to do that they aren't doing now. Another effective approach you can use is asking the child to think of someone their age whom they admire. Then, invite the child to think of something that person does that they wish they could do, and why, then ask the child if they wish to share these thoughts with you.

Now let's take a look at some ways to respond to the information you've received from the child during the case conceptualization process.

Helpful Therapist Responses

You will have noticed in the case conceptualization template that I ask about what matters to the child; this is because *choose what matters* is one of the six processes that make up the ACT Kidflex. When the child or their parent tells me about something the child did in the past that mattered to them, I make sure to give a big overreaction and say something like "That's amazing, I get so nervous about doing that; how did you manage to do that if you were feeling so worried?" or "Wow, that's incredible, I would be terrified to do that!"

I recommend that you allow the child to tell you about the activity they did. Then, when they have finished, ask them if they can remember how they felt at the time, and why they did the activity if their mind was telling them that they couldn't do it. This introduces the child (and their parent, if present) to the ACT Kidflex processes of *let it be* and *do what matters*. You can show the child through your facial expressions, with genuine animation, excitement, and awe, that you understand what a huge thing they did, especially given how nervous/worried/etc. they were.

An example of how I do this in my own work with children is as follows. If the child tells me that they went to a particular place (for example, a well-known theme park with a waterslide), I might ask for permission to look up the theme park on my phone, then show them (and their parent, if present) the photo and ask whether that is the correct place. This often really assists with rapport building, and I again give another big reaction, by saying something like "Wow, that really is amazing, I'm noticing that I'm feeling nervous in my body *(this introduces the* stay here *process of the ACT Kidflex)* just looking at the photos of that waterslide, and my *own* mind is telling me that I couldn't go on that slide *(this introduces the* let it go *process of the ACT Kidflex)*, but you actually went on it!" (I try to make sure that I don't use expressions like "butterflies in my tummy" because some children, such as autistic children, may interpret this literally and think you really do have butterflies in your stomach, or children may become worried that butterflies will enter their stomach.)

You can ask the child something like "How come if you were feeling so scared you didn't just turn around and walk away, and *not* go on the waterslide?" I allow the child to tell me what mattered to them (*choose what matters*), and inside, I'm saying a big "YES!!!" to myself and thinking that this child didn't let feeling afraid stop them from going on the waterslide. They have already done something that mattered to them (*do what matters*)—this is what ACT is all about!

After the child has finished telling me about the activity they did, I link doing the activity back to the problem or difficulty they are seeing me for by asking the child, "Why is this current problem or difficulty any different from when you went on the waterslide at the theme park?" It's important to just listen to the child, without interrupting them, debating with them, or trying to convince them of anything. This is because when using ACT, we don't ever try to convince anyone that what they are doing is wrong, or that we know better. I want the child to have what Louise Hayes refers to as an "ah ha" moment (L. Hayes, 2011) and realize that perhaps what they have been avoiding could actually be just like the waterslide—something that they can do, if they can find something about it that matters to them (*choose what matters*).

I inform the child (and their parent, if they are present) that the example they came up with (such as the waterslide) is going to help guide our work together. I add that if they choose to come back to see me (this lets the child know that they have a choice about whether to return to see you), my aim will be to try to help them with what they feel they cannot do at the moment, so that they can do things that matter to them (do what matters), even if their mind tells them that they can't because they are too nervous/scared/worried/sad/etc. (use the name of the problem or difficulty the child is seeing you for).

When getting to know the child and formulating your case conceptualization, it's important to ensure that before you finish the case conceptualization, you've obtained an understanding of:

- What's important to the child?
- What's the particular problem or difficulty?
- Is the way the child is trying to cope with the problem or difficulty stopping them from doing something that matters to them, and if so, what?

This will help you identify what the child might be missing out on as a result of their coping strategies. Bear in mind that in ACT, the particular issue itself is not a problem just because the child has it (for example, anxiety); rather, we look at the cost of the strategies the child has been using. This refers to the impact the child's coping strategies have on them.

HELPFUL HINT

It's important to actually ask the child whether the strategies they are using help them, or take them away from anything. Once you have this information, you can think about (without actually asking the child) whether or not the strategies the child is using are consistent with the overall goal of the ACT Kidflex: *I am flexible.*

Equipped with all of this valuable information from the case conceptualization, you'll now want to consider whether the child believes that *how* they have been trying to manage the problem or difficulty is working for them. This brings us to the concept of *creative hopelessness,* which we'll discuss next.

Creative Hopelessness

Creative hopelessness is not a process of the ACT Hexaflex or ACT Kidflex; rather, it's an acknowledgment by the child that what they have been doing to try to control or avoid the problem or difficulty, in order to try to manage it, has not been working. This is not a suggestion that the child is hopeless, or that their problem or difficulty is hopeless and cannot be helped.

Rather, the aim of creative hopelessness is for the child to stop trying strategies that are not working (Hayes et al., 1999) and be willing and open to learning and trying new ones in order to *choose what matters* and *do what matters* more consistently.

To help children evaluate their experiences and start to consider that their efforts to change how they feel might not have worked, ask the following questions:

- "What do you want, or how do you want things to be?"
- "What have you tried to manage or deal with this problem or difficulty?"
- "What happened—was what you did helpful?" (Hayes et al., 1999)

Through the case conceptualization process, the child may reveal that they have been trying to control how they feel and acknowledge that trying to use control is not working for them or not helping, and that they are missing out on things. In this case, creative hopelessness has already occurred, so you can make a note of it, but there's no need for you to do anything to *develop* creative hopelessness because the child is acknowledging that what they have tried doesn't work.

When creative hopelessness has *not* yet been developed, and the child feels that their efforts to try to control or avoid their problem or difficulty are working, or sometimes work, you could use a metaphor to engage the child in a discussion about the use of control or avoidance. When using metaphors with children, I prefer to make up my own instead of using traditional ACT metaphors that were developed for use with adults. When I first started learning about ACT, I *did* use traditional ACT metaphors with children, but I quickly realized that the children I worked with didn't understand the concepts. That might be because the concepts are too vague and are not based on examples that children can easily relate to.

HELPFUL HINT

It's important that any metaphors you use with children be very simple and practical so that children can easily picture the scenarios in their minds.

The following is an example of a metaphor I developed for use with children.

Needing the Restroom During a Movie

Imagine that you are sitting at the movie theater, watching a really great movie. You are greatly enjoying it, concentrating really well, and watching and listening to everything. Then you realize that you need to use the restroom! There's no way that you want to miss any of the movie by getting up and leaving the theater, especially because the restroom is at the opposite side of the building, so it will take a while to walk there and back. You decide that you will wait until the movie ends to go to the restroom, so you do everything you can to not think about needing the restroom, trying really hard to focus on the movie, and trying to ignore the sensation of really, really needing to go to the restroom.

You start wondering if you could walk out of the theater quickly, then run to the restroom, where there hopefully won't be a line of people waiting. You think about using the restroom quickly, and running back to the theater and returning to your seat as fast as you can. But wait, it might be hard to find your seat in the dark when you get back! You keep trying super hard not to think about needing to go, but the more you try to distract yourself, and not think about the restroom, the more that you need to go! If you walk out in the middle of the movie, you might miss something really great, that you can't catch up on, and you won't know what's happening when you return. In the time that you have sat there thinking about how to manage this, you have already been missing out on some of the movie, because you've been concentrating on how to solve the issue of needing the restroom, instead of watching the movie. Maybe you could stop trying not to think about needing the restroom, and instead, just notice that you need to use it, without trying not to think about it. Sometimes, the more we tell ourselves not to *think about something, the more we do think about it. Maybe a different way of dealing with our thoughts might be more helpful, which is actually the opposite of what your mind tells you to do.*

HELPFUL HINT

The Needing the Restroom During a Movie metaphor can also be adapted to watching a movie at home, but in this case, tell the child that the movie can't be recorded, paused, or stopped; otherwise they are likely to say that they will record, pause, or stop the movie in order to use the restroom, thereby not missing out on anything.

After completing the case conceptualization process and gaining an understanding of the history of the child's problem or difficulty (which may involve asking further questions and sometimes conducting a clinical interview as well), I introduce ACT to the child (and their parent, if present). I do this after the case conceptualization process to provide the child (and their parent, if appropriate) with information about how I plan to help the child using ACT. To do this, I give specific examples of what our sessions will focus on, including some possible goals that were identified through the case conceptualization process. Let's look now at how you can introduce ACT to children.

Introducing ACT to Children

Sometimes you will find that there is time in the first session to commence therapy after completing the case conceptualization. At other times, the case conceptualization will be very detailed and take up most of the first session (particularly if the child has experienced the problem or difficulty for a long time), in which case you will need to wait until the second session to commence therapy. Regardless of whether I commence therapy in the first or second session, I introduce ACT to children in the same manner in the first session.

The following example shows how I introduce ACT to children (and their parents when they are present); feel free to change or adapt this in any way you wish to.

Sample Script

In order to try to help children with their problems or difficulties, I use acceptance and commitment therapy, which we can shorten to ACT. ACT can also stand for accepting our thoughts and feelings, choosing what matters to us, and taking action to move toward those things. If you come back to see me, I will invite you to participate in some exercises during our sessions to teach you some new ways of coping with what you're dealing with, rather than only sitting and talking to you. I will always give you a choice of whether to take part in exercises—I'll never force you to participate, and if you choose to take part, I'll participate alongside you. For example, we might do some drawing or painting together, if that's something you'd like to try.

Some of what I'm going to teach you might be *quite* different from what you've heard from other people! I'm never going to try to change the way you think, and I won't suggest that you try to replace negative thoughts with positive thoughts. (*If I know that the child has undergone therapy using CBT with another therapist prior to seeing me, I will state that ACT is different from CBT just before saying that I won't try to change how they think.*) Also, I'll never ask you to convince me why your mind comes up with certain thoughts *(using the phrase "your mind comes up with" introduces the child to the* let it go *process).* One of the main things I'll focus on is trying to help you do some of the things that you've stopped doing or are unable to do, so that you don't miss out on things that matter to you *(this introduces the* do what matters *process).* How does all of that sound? Do you have any questions that you'd like to ask me?

> ## HELPFUL HINT
>
> Children usually want to see fairly quickly that you are going to be able to help them; otherwise they can be reluctant to return. As a result, even if time is limited, try to provide some strategies in the first session, even briefly, rather than only receiving information and telling the child that you will discuss strategies in the next session.

In a workshop I attended given by Kirk Strosahl (2015), he said that the greatest therapeutic change occurs between the first and second sessions. By introducing ACT in the first session, the child (and their parent, if present) receives an idea of what sessions using ACT will look like, which may help them decide whether they want to see you again, and you might also be able to give the child some helpful techniques that they can start using straight away.

Next, we'll look at several points to consider when introducing ACT to children—and throughout sessions.

Emphasize Talking About Safe Things

Whenever I talk to a child (and their parent) about choosing what matters, and not avoiding doing what matters due to their difficult thoughts and feelings, I always ensure that I stress that I'm *only* talking about doing safe things. This is because I don't want the child to leave the therapy room and mistakenly think that I told them not to listen to their mind when it tells them not to do something that could potentially be dangerous. To make this clear for the child, I give very specific examples of what safe things are, and I say that I'm not talking about risky activities such as riding a bike without a helmet, or bungee jumping, or crossing the road without walking to the crosswalk. I add that I'm only talking about things that we know are safe, even if they feel scared, nervous, or worried when doing them, such as trying out for the school running team or going to a new restaurant for pizza with their parents.

It can be useful to explain to the child that our mind's job is to try and protect us and keep us safe, as follows: "Sometimes our mind does a *really, really* good job of this. There are other times, however, when an action might feel really scary, like standing at the front of the class to give a presentation to the class and teacher *(and I disclose that this is something that I get nervous about)*, but giving a presentation in front of the class and teacher is not actually a *dangerous* activity."

Invite the Child to Become Their Own Superhero

By the end of the first session with the child, and having heard from them (and their parent) about their problem or difficulty and the toll it has had, I often have a visual image of the child wearing a scarf around their neck, and their mind holding the ends while bossing them around, saying in a big, loud voice, "Do this, don't do that, go here, don't go there," and so on.

When this is the case, sometimes I share my impressions, asking the child to correct me if I'm wrong. I add that they know their mind really, really well; in fact, they know their mind better than anyone else does, because, after all, they have lived with their mind every day for a very long time! When I share my impressions, the child will often respond by saying something like "Wow, how did you know that? That's *exactly* how it is!" I add that I would like to try and help them take back some of this power, and be able to choose for themself what they do and don't do, where they go and don't go, so they can become their own superhero. I find that most times, the child looks pretty pleased with this (and often surprised and excited by the idea) and says, "That would be great," or "Yes please." Often, this also appeals to the parent, who may turn to their child and affirm this.

HELPFUL HINT

You can start helping children become their own superhero by asking them to think about examples of when we *should not* listen to our mind and do what it tells us, and you can offer your own examples too.

When teaching children that we don't always have to listen to our mind, it works well to give them simple, everyday examples that they are likely to relate to (such as "Your mind has the thought that you should walk out of class and get your lunch when it tells you that you are hungry," or "Your mind says that you should go out to the school playground and play basketball in the middle of class when you are supposed to be learning").

Ask the child, "What would happen if you did what your mind told you?" You could also ask, "What would happen if I go home from my work in the middle of the day because my mind tells me that I'm tired and want to lie on the couch and watch TV, when I have children coming to my clinic for their appointments later that day?"

This is a good opportunity to have some fun, and often the child will laugh at some of the examples you both come up with, which is a great way to introduce them to ACT.

HELPFUL HINT

Children are more likely to remember therapy sessions if they had fun in the process, rather than it always being serious ... so go ahead and have some fun with them!

Convey That Therapy Is Voluntary

If the child is engaging in behaviors that they feel *are* helping them, which you feel are unhelpful (especially ones that are not consistent with ACT, such as avoidance), I recommend that you don't try to convince or persuade them that what they are doing is not helping them, or isn't working for them. The child might feel that they are absolutely fine and don't need any help (particularly if their parent has made the appointment without the child's agreement). If it is clear that the child doesn't want to return to see you again, despite your having tried really hard to engage them, you could suggest to the child and their parent that they take a few days to discuss whether the child wishes to return. This can help the child see that you respect their opinion and that they have choice about returning, which, in my experience, helps considerably with obtaining buy-in from the child for future sessions. I have seen a few children who were reluctant to return after the first session, and I was certain they wouldn't return, but they *did* return a few weeks later, were very receptive to receiving assistance, and willingly participated in sessions.

However, sometimes parents will want to book another appointment for their child to see you, rather than waiting a few days to decide. In this case, I might tell the child that I've helped lots of children with similar problems or difficulties, and I'd really like to try to help. I may then suggest to the child that they try one more appointment, and see how it goes. In some cases, the child agrees to this. But, if the child still doesn't wish to attend another appointment, I recommend to the parent that they give the child some time to think it over, rather than making a decision today. I also recommend that you let the child (and their parent) know that if they decide that they don't want to return, they *are* allowed to change their mind at a later stage, and you will be happy to see them at that time. The reason I do this is because the child might feel that if they return at a later stage (say in a few weeks or months), you might not want to help them.

If the child and their parent agree to take a few days to consider whether they wish to return, don't panic! And a few final points:

- Don't try to convince the child (or their parent) that you can help, or how wonderful ACT is—we are not trying to sell ACT!

- It is not our role as therapists to tell or convince children that their coping strategies are flawed or that they need help.
- You can say something like "It was really nice to meet you today. If I don't see you again, I wish you all the very best and hope that things improve for you."

Conclusion

You have completed the first session with the child, and their parent or caregiver has likely been in the therapy room for part of or all of the session. You have obtained a history of the problem or difficulty through developing a case conceptualization. You might have also conducted a clinical interview for a particular disorder, or you might plan to do that at the start of the second session. The information that you obtained about how the problem or difficulty is impacting the child, what they are missing out on, their coping strategies, what matters to them, and an action they might have done in the past that really mattered to them is going to be very important for you in order to plan the next session. In particular, you will use all of this information to work out which process or processes in the ACT Kidflex to start therapy with. The following chapter is about commencing therapy with children. It covers important matters to address in the second session—such as informed consent, voluntary participation, and self-disclosure by the therapist—and will start to guide you through the processes in the ACT Kidflex, beginning with *let it be* and *let it go*.

CHAPTER 3

Let It Be and Let It Go

In the first session with the child and their parent, you obtained a history of the problem or difficulty through developing a case conceptualization, and you introduced ACT to the child. Having done this, you are now aware of when and where the problem or difficulty shows up for the child, the strategies they've used to try to cope, the strategies the parent or caregiver has suggested, and what has been helpful and unhelpful for the child. You are now ready to begin the second session. In this chapter, you will read about important issues in working with children. We will then look at how we start therapy with the ACT Kidflex processes of *let it be* and *let it go,* and I'll show you lots of exercises you can select from when working with children. I'll also take you through a detailed case example, including recommendations for the child's parents. Let's get started.

Important Matters to Address in This Session

Before getting into the main focus of this session, you'll want to cover two essential topics:

(1) any missing information necessary for your case conceptualization, and (2) the issue of voluntary participation.

Through developing an ACT case conceptualization in the first session, I usually obtain a fairly clear picture of which process of the ACT Kidflex needs addressing first. However, sometimes when reviewing the case conceptualization after the first session, I haven't gained sufficient clarity and have a few more questions. When this occurs, I make a note of what I'm unsure about or what I haven't asked about, and I tell the child at the start of the second session that I've been thinking about what they told me last time we met, and there are a few things I'd like more information about. I ask these questions before proceeding with the ACT Kidflex because sometimes the child's responses may change which process I select to begin therapy with.

I recommend that when introducing every exercise, you always let the child know what's involved first, and that their participation is completely voluntary: they do not have to agree to participate, and you won't proceed without their consent. You can also tell the child that you will participate in every exercise that they do, which is very much in the ACT spirit of doing therapy *with* them, rather than *to* them.

HELPFUL HINT

> In my experience, children are more likely to agree to take part in exercises if they know that you're going to participate alongside them.

Where in the ACT Kidflex Do You Begin?

Every child is unique, so I don't always commence at the same place in the ACT Kidflex; rather, I attend to the process that seems the greatest priority. This is based on what I have identified—from using the case conceptualization template—as needing to be increased or improved. For example, if a child says, "I can't stand feeling like this; I wish it would just go away," then I consider starting therapy with *let it be*, and if a child says, "I spend ages trying to work out why this keeps happening to me, but I still don't know why," then I consider starting with *let it go*.

For each process, ask yourself why you need to address this process with this child, and what skills you want to teach them. If it's hard to answer those questions, try asking yourself why the child *doesn't* need to increase their skills in that process. In this way, your task is to convince yourself why you *don't* need to teach the child the particular process. This can help you identify whether you need to address all of the processes in the ACT Kidflex, or whether you might be including them because you feel that you *ought* to, simply because they are part of the ACT Kidflex.

HELPFUL HINT

You might not need to address every process of the ACT Kidflex with each child you work with.

I remember when I first started using ACT with children, I thought that I had to use all of the processes. I also thought that the more processes I addressed with clients, the better I was getting at using ACT. But over time, I've learned to become selective about which processes I choose to address with children. This is because some children may already have very good skills consistent with that process (for example, they might already be letting it be, or letting it go, or doing a great job of choosing what matters and doing what matters).

When there is more than one issue (for example, the child feels sad and also worries excessively), I say something like "I'm hearing that you feel sad and you also have worries; which one feels stronger—sadness or worries?" If the child identifies one as being stronger, I then ask if they would like to start with that one, and tell them that we may not have enough time to discuss the other issue today, but we will discuss it next time.

Although, as I've noted, there is no one right process of the ACT Kidflex to start working with, for the purpose of this book, we'll start with *let it be*. I'll guide you through how to introduce children to the *let it be* process and engage them in discussions.

Introducing Let It Be

Let it be refers to letting private experiences—such as painful or difficult thoughts, feelings, emotions, memories, urges, and physical sensations—just be there, without trying to do anything with them, like get rid of them, avoid them, replace them, or look for evidence for and against them. When we don't try to do anything with them, we just allow them to be there, letting them be.

Very often, the child has been working hard (sometimes together with a well-meaning parent) to do everything they can to get rid of the problem or difficulty or avoid it. *Let it be* is often the appropriate place to start, and might in fact be the opposite of what the child has been doing (and sometimes the opposite of what their parent has been suggesting).

The *let it be* and *let it go* processes work really well together, and in some exercises (such as the blowing bubbles exercise later in this chapter), you can combine them instead of using them separately.

Things Don't Always Turn Out How We Expect

To introduce *let it be,* you could start a discussion by saying, "We cannot control everything; sometimes we are forced to stop doing things we usually do, or things that we like to do." Ask the child, "Can you think of any examples of this?"

If the child can't think of any, you could use the following examples to explain:

- Being unwell with a fever is a time when you might not be able to attend school, or, during COVID-19, some schools closed for a while to prevent the virus from spreading.

- If your friend invites you to their house and then finds out that they are going on vacation, they will need to reschedule for a different time.

- You and your parent might plan a trip to your favorite bakery and arrive there to find that it's closed.

Then, invite the child to think of some examples of when they had to stop doing something that they usually did, or something that they liked or wanted to do. After the child shares an example, you might also share an appropriate example from your own life, adding that it was something that you were disappointed about, and you accepted it.

You could also add something like "Sometimes we can't control things, and sometimes things don't turn out the way we expected, and that's okay."

Encouraging the child to think about a time when things didn't turn out the way they had thought they would, and asking them if they would like to share their example with you, can be a helpful way of generating discussion about control. If the child does share an example, you might like to respond with an appropriate example of your own, and add something to the effect of "We don't always know the answers about how things are going to be, and that's okay."

Can We Tell Our Minds Not to Think About Something?

An effective way to illustrate the *let it be* process is by asking the child if they think that we can tell our own mind *not* to think about something, and, if they try to do this, does their mind think about it even more or less? This often generates the child's curiosity and makes them eager to find out.

The following example is one that most children are likely to be able to consider: "Have you ever noticed that when you are really thirsty, if you try to tell yourself not to think about being thirsty, you probably feel even *more* thirsty?"

You can also generate more conversation by using the example we read about in chapter 2 in the section on creative hopelessness. Ask the child: "What happens if you are at the movies *(or they can pretend that they are at the movies)* and are really interested in the movie, following every scene very carefully, and then you realize that you need to use the restroom? Can you tell yourself *not* to think about needing to use the restroom? If you try this, what do you think might happen?"

Then, ask the child if they can think of any examples of when they *can* tell their mind not to think about something, or when they can tell their mind to *stop* thinking of something.

Just Noticing Our Thoughts and Feelings

After you've had a discussion with the child about whether we can tell our minds not to think about something, you can introduce the idea that instead of trying to tell our mind what *not* to think about, we can let all our thoughts and feelings be, just by noticing them (Hayes & Smith, 2005) and not trying to fight them. You can emphasize the following to the child:

We can allow whatever thoughts and feelings that show up to just be

there, without trying to do anything with them.

On the following page, you will find a worksheet that you can invite the child to complete during the therapy session to help them better understand the concept of *let it be*. This worksheet, along with all of the other worksheets in this book, can be downloaded in color from the website for this book: http://www.newharbin ger.com/49760. For children who have difficulties with reading, writing, or spelling, you could read the questions to them and offer to write their answers on the worksheet for them. If they don't wish to complete the worksheet during the session, you can tell them that's okay and give them the option of taking it home. (If they agree to, it helps to let their parent or caregiver know you have given the child a worksheet to complete at home, and you can suggest that they might wish to remind their child at a suitable time to complete it, or supervise them while they complete it.)

Worksheet 1:
Letting Our Thoughts Be

What thoughts do you try to tell your mind *not* to think about?

_____

_____

Is this easy or difficult to do?

_____

_____

What are one or two thoughts you could try to leave alone and just let be, *without* trying to tell your mind not to think about them?

_____

_____

Now draw a picture of yourself having one of these thoughts and letting it be, *without* trying to do anything with it:

HELPFUL HINT

If the child completes a worksheet in a session, ask them if they would like to take it home. If they would like to, ask their permission to photograph or photocopy it, and let them know that you would like to put the copy in their file.

Now we'll go over some exercises for the *let it be* process that you can do with children during therapy sessions.

Let It Be Exercises

After suggesting the Letting Our Thoughts Be worksheet (for the child to complete in session or at home), it's a great time to invite the child to take part in an exercise to experience what *let it be* means. The first one, below, is a fun, short exercise that most children enjoy.

Don't Think About Chocolate Cake
(Hayes et al., 1999)

One of the reasons I really enjoy doing this exercise with children is that you can be pretty creative with it and change the wording any way you like. I've found that most children are usually willing to participate, probably because chocolate cake is something that many children can easily imagine, and it might also sound interesting to them. If the child doesn't wish to participate, you can tell them that it's okay, they don't have to, and if they'd like to come back to it another time, they can let you know.

HELPFUL HINT

I want to assure you that with all ACT exercises, you don't have to follow an exact script, word for word. You can adapt the exercises, injecting them with your own creativity, rather than having to rehearse and follow someone else's words. This is one of the things that I love most about using ACT. Though I was nervous about adapting exercises when I first began learning ACT, I soon realized that I actually felt much more authentic when using ACT than when I used other therapies where I hadn't been encouraged to be creative and adapt exercises myself.

An example of how I use the Don't Think About Chocolate Cake exercise is something like this:

"Let your mind think about whatever it wants to. Whatever thoughts it wants to think of, let them show up, but whatever you do, do *not* let yourself think about chocolate cake! Don't think about what a piece of freshly baked chocolate cake would smell like, and taste like, especially if it had chocolate frosting on it, and perhaps some warm chocolate sauce dripping down it.

Think about anything else, but do not think about chocolate cake!"

After you have taken the child through this exercise, you can then ask them what happened for them during the exercise, and what they thought of. If they say that they were thinking about chocolate cake, you can add that you yourself were imagining a huge piece of chocolate cake, and you even noticed the saliva in your mouth while you were talking!

Some children will report that they were able to tell their minds not to think about chocolate cake. When this occurs, don't argue with the child's experience, and don't try to convince them otherwise; rather, you can let them know this happens for lots of people, so they don't feel that there is something wrong with them or that they couldn't do the exercise properly.

This exercise can help develop children's understanding of *let it be,* and how useful using *let it be* actually is, by experiencing that it's actually really hard to tell their mind not to have a certain thought—and, moreover, that if they try *not* to think about something, they may have the thought even more! If the child informs you that they weren't able to tell their mind not to think about chocolate cake, and if you experienced the same, I recommend telling the child that you *also* couldn't control your mind.

HELPFUL HINT

It may be helpful for the child to hear you normalize just how hard it is to try to control your own thoughts. This can be a really powerful and effective way to teach the *let it be* process because, by showing the child that you're human too and that you have the same difficulties they have, they often become more open and willing to consider a new way of dealing with their thoughts.

Note that *let it be* and *let it go* are complementary and go hand in hand: for example, you can let a thought just be there, without trying to do anything with it, and then you can let it go. So although I've listed the next four exercises under "Let It Be Exercises," they can all be used together with *let it go* exercises. We will begin with an art exercise, followed by a practical exercise to teach children how to let their thoughts be, then an exercise that shows children how our thoughts are created, and finally an easy exercise for relating to our thoughts and feelings. As with worksheets that are completed in therapy sessions, for all art exercises, I recommend asking the child if they would like to take their work home, and if they would, I suggest that you ask their permission to photograph or photocopy their work in order to have a copy for your file.

Invitation to Our Thoughts

I've found that a great way of introducing both *let it be* and *let it go* to children is through art exercises. For this art exercise, invite the child to draw a backpack, tote bag, or handbag and write an invitation to the thoughts, feelings, and physical sensations they have been struggling with to come with them on their journey. You can suggest that the child pretends that the thoughts, feelings, and physical sensations can ride with them in their bag, or even help them carry it (Coyne, 2011).

Glitter Bottle

To make a glitter bottle, you will need a small plastic bottle with a lid and some coarse glitter in a few different colors (if the glitter is too fine it won't sink to the bottom and then the exercise won't be as powerful). Having some glitter shapes as well also works great. Fill the bottle with water and add one drop only of a light color food dye. If the food dye is too dark, you won't be able to see the glitter, so you'll need to spill out most of the water and refill the bottle with water to dilute it. Then add a drop of dishwashing liquid (this helps the glitter float), followed by the glitter.

Having a pre-prepared glitter bottle in the session is often a great way of generating the child's interest in teaching them about *let it be*. I usually contact the child's parent before the session to ask what the child's favorite color is, then make a glitter bottle in that color to increase the likelihood of the child being interested in the exercise.

I introduce this exercise as follows:

"Is trying to push away your thoughts about *(include the reason the child is seeing you)* helpful, or do they come back again?" Make sure that you include in this question the specific reason the child is seeing you; otherwise, they might not see the exercise as relevant, and then not be interested. (Allow the child to respond.)

Next, pick up the bottle and turn it downward and upward a few times until the glitter has been shaken up and is moving around. Say, "The glitter is like your thoughts, and the bottle is like your mind. What happens when we turn the bottle upside down and try to push the glitter away? Does that help get the glitter to move back to the bottom of the bottle, or is holding the bottle still a better way?" (Allow the child to respond.)

Say, "Sometimes trying to push away our thoughts can just make them come back again, so instead, we can just notice what's happening in our mind (Hayes & Smith, 2005) and let our thoughts be, which can help our thoughts settle down in our minds, just like the glitter settles in the bottle when we let the bottle be."

If you are using a glitter bottle in a face-to-face session, I recommend offering the child to take it home to keep, so they can use the glitter bottle on their own at home to help them practice letting their thoughts be.

Jumbled Letters

I developed this exercise for use with Liam, a seven-year-old boy who was extremely afraid of storms. When there was heavy rain, he worried that there would also be thunder and lightning. If Liam was at home during a storm, he would run into his bedroom and cower under the duvet until the storm stopped. If he was in the car during a storm, he would be terrified about being in a car crash, and if he was at a shopping center or a friend's home during a storm, he would insist on looking up the weather map online, and would only agree to return home if he was certain that the storm had finished.

This exercise can be done with children with a specific fear (in this example, storms) who are able to spell what they fear most. You will need to print out the letters of the word in enlarged font, with one letter per page. Purposely mix up the order of the letters (so that they don't spell anything), and ask the child if they are happy to participate in an exercise looking at letters of the alphabet, which you will place on the floor.

You can take turns with the child to jumble up the letters differently each time, with both of you trying to pronounce the non-word—which can be lots of fun. Each time you and the child take turns jumbling up the letters, ask the child to look at the letters and then let you know how they are feeling in their body. Liam and I had great fun mixing up the letters into different combinations, and then he stated with excitement, "Mrost spells storm!" I replied, "That's correct, these letters do make the word 'storm'; how are you feeling in your body now that the word 'storm' is spelled out?" (If the child is unable to work out what the letters spell, and you place the letters in their correct order to create the word, you could also ask how the child is feeling in their body now that the word is spelled out.)

This exercise helps children to experience that their thoughts and feelings cannot hurt them, which can promote the process of *let it be*. You might conclude that just as the jumbled letters can't hurt us, the word "storm" (or whatever word has been spelled out) can't hurt us either. You can then say something like the following, so that the child can see the link between this exercise and learning about the *let it be* process:

"Our thoughts and feelings start off as letters of the alphabet, which are put together to form words, which cannot actually hurt us, no matter how scared/worried/sad/etc. *(use the problem or difficulty that the child is seeing you for)* we feel."

Saying Hello to Our Thoughts and Feelings

In this exercise, you can suggest to children that they say something like "Hello sadness/worries/scared/etc., it's nice to see you" to their difficult thoughts and feelings when they show up, and they can also imagine giving their thoughts and feelings a pat on the shoulder (Twohig, 2014).

When teaching this exercise to children, you can also inject some humor, being careful not to poke fun at the child's thoughts and feelings, but instead by using great animation and enthusiasm in your voice. To do this, I recommend that you use a neutral example of your own, rather than the problem or difficulty the child is experiencing. For example, I might say that I get nervous cooking a new meal for my family, so I could say, "Hello worries about my cooking, it's really great to see you." Or, "Hello worries about my cooking, you are looking fabulous today!"

This exercise teaches the child to let their thoughts and feelings be—instead of getting rid of them, or trying to change them, or challenging them—and it also teaches children that they don't have to *fear* their thoughts and feelings. This is probably the *opposite* of what the child expects to hear from you, as most people think that difficult thoughts and feelings are harmful, and as result, they look for a way to reduce them and get rid of them.

Some more examples of saying hello to your thoughts and feelings that you could use in sessions with children are:

- "Hello worries, it's so nice to see you again!"
- "Hi scared, you look great today!"
- "Welcome back sadness, it's wonderful to see you!"

You could tell the child that this strategy goes along with just noticing all of our thoughts (Hayes & Smith, 2005) and feelings, without having to do anything to try to get rid of them. You might also wish to remind the child that earlier on, we experienced that sometimes it can be really hard to get rid of our thoughts and feelings or to tell ourselves *not* to think or feel something.

HELPFUL HINT

Remember from the previous chapter that children are more likely to remember what they did in therapy if they have some fun in the process. Saying hello to our thoughts and feelings, and even welcoming them, is likely to come as quite a surprise to the child, who might respond with laughter, especially if you

> are using humor about your own struggle rather than the child's.

We've completed looking at exercises for *let it be,* and will now look at exercises for *let it go.*

Introducing Let It Go

Let it go refers to stepping back and getting some separation between us and our thoughts, so that we are not stuck or attached to them. We are not trying to get rid of our thoughts, or reduce how often they show up, or replace them; rather, *let it go* involves being able to see them for what they are—just thoughts—without letting them have lots of power over us.

I've noticed that several parents of the children I work with ask that I help their child to be able to move on quickly from arguments with friends, siblings, and parents; bounce back from feeling disappointed, or angry, or frustrated; and not carry a grudge. Teaching children the *let it go* process can be very helpful for them and reduce the amount of conflict they have with others.

We introduce *let it go* through exercises, of which there are many you can do with children. Tell the child, "We are going to practice seeing our thoughts as just thoughts, rather than having to believe that everything our mind tells us is true."

Let It Go Exercises

I've included a broad range of *let it go* exercises below: some of these are very simple ones that children can quickly and easily practice outside of sessions. There's also an experiential exercise, as well as drawings and fun interactive exercises you and the child can do together. Let's start with a widely used ACT exercise that works very well with children.

I'm Having the Thought That

You can introduce this exercise to children by suggesting that they say the phrase "I'm having the thought that..." (Hayes & Smith, 2005), followed by a thought. Give the child an example of how they might do this, such as: "I'm having the thought that I'm bored," or "I'm having the thought that I can't do this." I recommend giving the child a neutral example (such as boredom) and also one that relates to a difficulty that children are likely to have (for example, "I'm having the thought that I don't understand my schoolwork" or "I'm having the thought that I'm not sure what to do at recess at school today").

In this way, you are teaching the child how they can use this exercise for everyday thoughts that don't bother them much—which might increase the likelihood of the child taking this on as part of their coping toolkit—as well as for more troubling thoughts. After you give the child some examples, ask them if they can think of a few different ways of using the phrase "I'm having the thought that...," which they might like to share with you. Then, ask the child how they think they could try to start using this phrase, and suggest that perhaps they could come up with some specific examples for using it at home, school, and anywhere else it might be helpful.

This exercise helps children to let their thoughts go by creating some distance between them and their thoughts. When they use the phrase "I'm having the thought that...," often their thoughts don't trouble them as much, and they start to be able to see their thoughts just as words—that they don't have to respond to, react to, or do anything with.

Naming the Story

This is another *let it go* exercise I often use that helps to create distance between children and their thoughts, so that they're not as distressed or overwhelmed by their thoughts. The exercise involves rephrasing the thought when it shows up so that it's like the title of a story (Harris, 2007). You can explain to the child that they can think about their thought as though it's part of a story, and ask them to come up with a name for their story.

I always assure children that there's no wrong or right name, and that I won't judge the title they come up with. I find that it's helpful for children if you first come up with an example of your own so they understand the idea, for example, "Here's the 'worrying about how I'm going to perform when I play tennis this week' story," or "Here's 'the lady who was worried she wouldn't do a good job baking her son a birthday cake' story." If the child isn't sure what to name their own story, you could give them an example related to their problem or difficulty, such as "Here's the 'who am I going to talk to at school' story," or "Here's 'the boy who didn't like going to camp' story."

Once the child has come up with a name for their story, you can invite them to imagine how those words would sound if they were a voice-over in a movie trailer; then ask if they would like to have a go at saying the name of the story in a way that sounds like a voice-over. This often brings some fun and lightheartedness into this exercise. If the child agrees, after they have shared their own voice-over, you could reciprocate by sharing a name for your own story (for example, "Here's the 'I'm not great at jigsaw puzzles' story"), then you can say it like a voice-over.

If you use an exaggerated voice when expressing a voice-over for your own thought, the child will probably enjoy hearing you do this, which can make the exercise quite fun, especially if the child then reciprocates by using an exaggerated voice for their own thoughts too. You'll notice that I say a few times in this book that children are more likely to remember exercises if they've had fun doing them, which is also true for this exercise.

Thanking Your Mind

Similar to the Naming the Story exercise above, this *let it go* exercise involves thanking your mind for such an interesting thought (Luoma et al., 2007). This also helps children to let go of thoughts so that they are less impacted or weighed down by them. To introduce this exercise to a child, give them an example of a thought you might thank your mind for. I recommend that when you are giving the child an example, you try to use an animated voice, and then ask the child if they wish to come up with their own example.

An example that you could give the child is "Thank you mind for telling me that no one is going to have fun at my fortieth birthday party;

what a fascinating thought—in fact it's the most interesting thing I've heard all day!" I find that when I use this exercise with children and share an example of my own, they usually smile or laugh. This exercise can help facilitate *let it go* by making the thought feel lighter, which then results in children becoming less burdened or worried by their thoughts.

Waves on the Ocean

I adapted the following experiential *let it go* exercise from Hayes and Smith (2005). For this exercise, give the child the option of either closing their eyes or choosing a spot on the floor to focus on, so that they are not looking around the room and unable to concentrate. As discussed earlier in this chapter, I recommend that you don't read out a script. Instead, try to talk the child through the exercise, slowly, and feel free to adapt it, rather than having to recall it exactly as it is written. It doesn't have to be perfect! If your mind comes up with the thought that you might not be able to recall it exactly as it is written, or that you are worried you will make a mistake, just notice that thought, and have a go anyway. You are more likely to be authentic and provide the child with a richer, more meaningful experience if you aren't looking at a piece of paper. Remember that the goal of the ACT Kidflex is *I am flexible*, so this is also a good way to show the child that you yourself are flexible, and that the exercise does not have to be done perfectly.

Sample Script for Waves on the Ocean

Imagine that it's summer, and you go to the beach. The sun is shining, and the sand is warm, but it's not too hot, so you won't burn your feet if you walk barefoot. Walk over to the water, and stand in it, so that your feet are just covered by the water. Notice how blue the ocean is, with the loud, crashing of the waves as they break on the sand, rolling in to where you are standing. Notice the feel of the sand in between your toes, and under your feet, as they start to sink a little into the sand. Notice how cool the water feels as it laps around your feet and ankles. Notice what your mind is thinking, and when a wave rolls in, watch it, and as it comes closer, imagine that you put a thought onto that wave, and watch it roll back out to sea. Notice your next thought, and when another wave comes in, put your thought onto that wave—it's okay if you are having more than one thought, you can put them all on the one wave—and watch it roll away. When you are ready, open your eyes, and come back to being in the room here with me (when doing this exercise online, I say, "Come back to being here online with me").

Ideas for Discussion. After pausing for a few moments and allowing the child time to sit with their thoughts and feelings and get used to bringing their attention back to being in your consulting room (or in their own home if therapy is done online), you can gently ask the child

1.   what the exercise was like for them (do not ask "How did you find that exercise?" or they make take you literally and reply that they didn't find it—you did);

2.   whether it was difficult to imagine being at the beach and trying to put their thoughts on to waves (if they tell you that they were unable to imagine the beach and ocean, say, "That's okay, sometimes that happens," and ask them if they would like to share what they were thinking during the exercise); and

3.   whether they might like to practice the exercise at home, school, or somewhere else and whether there are situations where they think it could be helpful.

HELPFUL HINT

When I do experiential exercises with children, I begin by letting them know that there's no wrong or right way to do the exercise, so if they like the exercise and want to do it on their own, at home, school, or somewhere else, it's perfectly fine to mix it up, and they don't have to recall it exactly as I have said it.

Writing Thoughts on Drawings

For this exercise, the child can choose one of the options below to draw. On the drawing, they can write some of the different thoughts their mind often comes up with, or thoughts that they struggle with (you might like to suggest that they draw the objects large enough so they can write a different thought on each object).

You can also give the child the option of drawing something of their own choice if they prefer instead of choosing from the options below.

Objects to Draw

- waves on the ocean
- candies in a jar
- fruit salad in a bowl
- skyscrapers in a city
- ducks swimming in a lake
- surfboards on a beach
- cows in a meadow
- sunflowers in a field
- shells on the sand
- flowers in a vase
- trees in a forest
- books on a shelf

As an alternative to drawing these objects, the child can draw a picture of themself with a speech bubble for their thoughts and write their thoughts in the speech bubble.

Blowing Bubbles

This is one of my favorite exercises, and is often a lot of fun. The exercise encompasses both *let it be* and *let it go,* and I have found that children of all ages (even the teenage siblings of child clients) as well as their parents really enjoy it. It is also a good way of developing rapport, especially with children who might feel uncomfortable with the therapy process. If the child's sibling and/or parent or caregiver is sitting in the waiting area, if appropriate, you could ask the child if they would like to invite them to join this exercise.

To do this exercise, I use a few small plastic bottles of bubbles bought from a dollar store (I always have a few extra bottles on hand in case one doesn't work or gets spilled), and I invite the child (and their sibling/parent/caregiver if the child wants them to join the exercise) to go outside. You can also do this exercise inside if you prefer, but I find that children enjoy doing it outside as they can watch the bubbles blow in the wind. I give the child (and any others, if present) a bottle of bubbles, and I take a bottle for myself too.

Suggested Instructions. Introduce the exercise by saying something like the following: "We are going to take turns noticing what our mind is telling us. First, we are going to say a thought aloud; then we are going to blow the bubbles once. We are not going to do anything to try to get rid of the bubbles, so we will not be pushing the bubbles away, or popping them, or stomping on them; we are just going to watch them. Then the other person will have their turn to say their thought, aloud, and blow once. We will keep taking turns to do this."

You can begin the exercise by saying something like "I'm having the thought that I'm not sure what I'm going to cook for dinner tonight" and then blow bubbles. You can intersperse the types of thoughts you express to the child, balancing neutral ones with some difficult thoughts (for example, "My mind is telling me that I'm not doing a very good job of blowing bubbles today"). This will show the child that you have struggles too, and that our minds have a range of thoughts, from everyday thoughts about small things that don't impact us, to thoughts that might trouble us.

After the child lets you know that they've had enough of the exercise (or they've finished their bottle), you can return to the consulting room with them (and suggest that their sibling/parent/caregiver return to the waiting area).

Invite the child to discuss their experience of the exercise, and relate the discussion back to what they're seeing you for. You could ask how they might be able to use what they experienced in the exercise for their problem or difficulty, and ask if there might be anything that could make it hard to try noticing their thoughts without trying to do anything with them. Ask the child if they would like to take the bottle of bubbles home to keep.

Singing Our Thoughts

I find that children of all ages enjoy this fun *let it go* exercise and often report that their thoughts feel lighter or less bothersome afterward. You can invite the child to participate in an exercise where they try putting their thoughts to the tune of a song (Hayes & Smith, 2005) and singing it. If the child agrees, you can do this first (with appropriate disclosure), then invite the child to have a turn. Before I sing, I usually tell the child, "I'm having the thought that you will probably notice very quickly that I am terrible at singing." This shows your own use of the *let it go* strategy "I'm having the thought that" and doing the exercise anyway, even when your mind has thoughts about being negatively judged. For example, I might sing the following, where I have changed some lyrics in the song "The

Sounds of Silence" (Simon & Garfunkel, 1964) to:

"Hello self-doubt my old friend, it's nice to see you again

You show up about my counseling skills, you say I'm not good enough

And I say, thanks mind."

Just be aware that most children won't recognize the tune if they aren't familiar with Simon and Garfunkel, but that's okay!

Musical Thoughts Using Instruments

This *let it go* exercise, which I learned in a workshop given by Laurie Greco and Debra Emery (Greco & Emery, 2010), can be very enjoyable and effective for children (as well as therapists). Like the Singing Our Thoughts exercise above, I have also used this exercise with great success with both neurotypical and autistic children.

It's helpful to have a range of instruments to give the child a choice, as this may help generate their interest in the exercise. I have used instruments from my children's toy collection, or, if you work in an organization that uses music, such as a hospital or school, you might ask to borrow some instruments. I have used inexpensive maracas from a dollar store, tambourines, symbols, castanets, and bells. If you are unable to access instruments, you could make your own, using a small plastic bottle filled with some uncooked rice or dried beans. You could also tap unopened cans with metal spoons, or tap a table with a metal spoon or ruler, or shake a bunch of keys.

Suggested Instructions. Start by showing the child the instruments and informing them that if they would like to take part, you will both take turns singing a difficult thought of your own while playing some instruments. I recommend giving the child an example of an appropriate thought of your own so they understand what you are referring to.

You can inform the child that it's not a singing competition, and that there's no right or wrong way to do this, and you can also add that you are already noticing your mind telling you that you aren't going to do a good job singing and playing with the instruments.

If the child agrees to participate, you could go first by singing an appropriate struggle of your own (for example, "I'm not smart enough," or "I'm really bad at baking; I always burn the cake," or "I'm not a very patient mommy"), while you wave and shake the instruments around. Then you can invite the child to have a turn. Allow the child to decide when to finish—the key is to have fun while doing this exercise.

Afterward, you can invite the child to have a discussion with you about their experience doing the exercise, and whether they think that they might like to try musical thoughts on their own in the future, even if they do not have instruments.

Watching Cars Drive Past

Before doing this exercise, you can introduce the child to the idea of noticing all your thoughts, and letting them come and go, like cars that drive past your house (Harris, 2009), without trying to do anything with them. You can let the child know that our thoughts might come and go, and return again later, and that's okay!

I developed the following exercise when working with Dale, who is autistic. I realized quickly that the suggestion of letting his thoughts come and go like cars didn't make much sense to him, evidenced by the confused look on his face. When I suggested that we look out the window to watch the cars driving past the building, Dale quickly jumped up and walked over to the window. His mother was in the room, and she informed me that Dale loves cars. He delighted in demonstrating his knowledge of cars and being able to correctly name the brand when the cars were quite far away. Dale remained engaged in this exercise for quite some time and was noticeably more relaxed as a result of participating. Because this exercise was very enjoyable for Dale, it really helped me to build rapport with him.

Suggested Instructions. If your office is by a window, preferably on a busy road, you can invite the child to stand by the window, and *just notice* all of the cars that drive past, and comment on the color of the car (and brand if, like Dale, they think they can recognize it).

The task here is to just notice the car, then just notice the next one, and so on, without getting caught up in judgments about any particular cars.

You can guide the child to just notice each car, and then the next car, and if their mind starts making judgments about whether they like the car, whether it's old or new, or whether it's a good or bad car, they can try to bring their attention back to just noticing. For example, "There's a red car, there's a Jeep," and so on.

After this exercise, you can invite the child to complete the following worksheet, which is available for download in color from http://www.newharbinger.com/49760.

Worksheet 2: Noticing Our Thoughts Like Cars Driving Past

Spend a few minutes noticing each thought your mind comes up with, without making any judgments about the thoughts. Now write some of your thoughts here:

_____

_____

_____

_____

_____

What are two thoughts your mind often has that you could practice just noticing, without judging them?

_____

_____

We can notice our thoughts like cars driving past—just noticing the color, shape, and size of the car without judging the car. Draw some cars below, then write some of the thoughts your mind often comes up with, writing a different thought above each car:

With any of these exercises, toward the end of session, you can suggest some home tasks for the child to do in order to practice the exercises they completed in the therapy session. I always make sure *not* to use the term "homework," which is often associated with school. Instead, I use the term "home tasks" so the child doesn't feel that they are receiving homework (which they might not be motivated to do). I recommend asking the child, "Is there anything that might make it hard for you to do this?" By addressing any barriers or obstacles the child can identify that might make it difficult to start trying the new techniques, you'll increase the likelihood of their actually trying the task.

HELPFUL HINT

I recommend bringing the parent (where appropriate) into the consulting room for a few minutes toward the end of the child's session to inform them of the task that you recommend the child try, as well as any actions the parent can do at home that will remind the child of what they've learned in the session.

You now have a host of *let it be* and *let it go* techniques and exercises to choose from to incorporate into your sessions. Let's look at how I used some of these techniques with one of my clients and what recommendations I gave to his parents.

Case Example: Bobby, Nine Years Old

Bobby's parents contacted me during the first COVID-19 lockdown, when his school was required to close for face-to-face learning for a few months. Bobby had a long history of anxiety. His mother usually drove him and his two brothers to school, parked her car, and walked them in. However, on the last day of school before the closure, parents were required to drop their children at school, without walking them in. The teachers at the school gate wore medical masks that day, which Bobby was not prepared for. When he saw the teachers, he felt frightened and cried, and he did not want to leave his mom's car.

At Bobby's parents' request, I met with them once without him, prior to his first therapy session, to obtain a history of Bobby's difficulties. Their goals for Bobby were for him to learn strategies to manage his anxiety and develop greater independence and confidence. I saw Bobby twice before he returned to school, and, due to COVID-19, all sessions were conducted online. Based on my clinical assessment, Bobby met the criteria for a diagnosis of generalized anxiety disorder. To help Bobby manage his anxiety, I used *exposure* (this refers to the client doing things that they are fearful of, or struggle with, in a safe way in therapy sessions), which involved asking Bobby to recall the last day of school, talk about his memories of arriving at school, and sit with his thoughts and feelings, without doing anything with them *(let it be)*.

Using Let It Be and Let It Go with Bobby

Below is a transcript from one of my sessions with Bobby that shows how an exposure technique helped him to experience the *let it be* process. Toward the end of the transcript, I briefly addressed the *let it go* process.

Therapist: Bobby, you have told me that there are some things that worry you. What is the thing that you worry about the most, or your biggest worry?

Bobby: Change.

Therapist: I know that lots and lots of children, teenagers, and adults worry about change too. What is it about change that worries you?

Bobby: That I'm not used to it, and I don't know what is going to happen.

Therapist: Can you try and think about a situation where you went somewhere and felt really worried, because it was not how you imagined it would be?

Bobby: Yes, a few days before home schooling started, I went to school with my brothers, and when we got there everything looked very different: the teachers were wearing white masks and parents weren't allowed into school. I got really scared and didn't want to get out of mom's car, and I was crying.

Therapist: It sounds like in those situations where things look different from how you expected them to be, your mind does a bit of a panic and gets super worried. Does that sound right?

Bobby: Yes.

Therapist: You are doing really, really well. Could we do an exercise now where I ask you to think about that time and I talk to you about what you've told me?

Bobby: Sure.

Therapist: If you like, you could shut your eyes, or if you don't want to, you can choose a point on the floor to focus on, just so that you can concentrate on the exercise (*Bobby closed his eyes).* I want you to concentrate on how you are feeling in your body, and imagine that you are in Mom's car, and she pulls up at school and you see the teachers wearing masks covering their noses and mouths. Try and notice how it feels in your chest, throat, and tummy as you imagine yourself in Mom's car. Try and think about some of the thoughts and feelings that your mind came up with.

Bobby: It was weird, but what was *really* weird was that no parents were allowed to walk their kids into school. When we went into class that morning all the chairs were set up differently, usually the chairs and tables are pushed together, but that day each table only had one chair at it, and the tables were spread out so no one was sitting close to each other. When I walked into the class everyone was sitting on the carpet, but very far away from each other.

Therapist: So there were lots of changes for you that morning. Good job remembering all these things; you are doing really well. So how did you get yourself out of Mom's car so that you could walk into the school on your own that day?

Bobby: I didn't walk in on my own. Because I was so upset, Mom drove me around the streets near school a few times and told me that she would come back at lunchtime to pick me up. We drove back to school and my teacher saw me in Mom's car crying, she came to the car to comfort me, and then walked alongside me into school.

Therapist: How is it feeling in your body right now remembering that morning?

Bobby: Bad. I remember I was crying, and I have some butterflies in my tummy.

Therapist: I would like to teach you something that can be helpful for other children when they have worries, and sometimes I use it too. Would that be okay?

Bobby: Sure.

At this point, I did some *let it go* exercises: asking Bobby what colors he imagined his feelings were, what size and shapes they looked like (Hayes & Smith, 2005), and, if he could imagine them as animals, what animals they would be.

Therapist: When you go back to school, how do you think you're going to feel when Mom's car arrives at the car drop-off area?

Bobby: I will feel a bit weird; it will probably be the same as when I went to school before the lockdown, but this time I'll be prepared for the teachers wearing masks.

Therapy: Do you normally get a bit nervous or a bit worried on the first day of school?

Bobby: Yes.

Therapist: I work at a school, and this also happens to me *(pauses, giving Bobby time to let it be, without having to do anything with this thought).* How is your tummy feeling now?

Bobby: Better, it's like the butterflies are lying down.

Using a Glitter Bottle with Bobby

Because Bobby and I worked together online, I emailed his parents prior to the session and provided them with easy-to-follow instructions on how to make a glitter bottle. This way he could have his own for use in the session and also be able to practice using it at home afterward. (I asked them not to show the glitter bottle to him until our session so that he would not be disinterested in it during the session.) Instructions for how to make a glitter bottle and a script for this exercise can be found earlier in this chapter under Let It Be Exercises.

The following transcript illustrates how the glitter bottle exercise further helped Bobby to learn the concept of *let it be*.

Therapist: Do you think trying to push the worries away makes them go away, or do they come back again?

Bobby: Sometimes they go away but sometimes they don't.

Therapist: Have a look at the glitter bottle; the glitter is a bit like worries and the bottle is a bit like your mind. When we turn the bottle upside down and try to push the glitter away, what happens?

Bobby: The glitter falls and flies around the bottle.

Therapist: Does the glitter go away?

Bobby: No, it just moves somewhere else.

Therapist: (*invites Bobby to hold the bottom of the glitter bottle, without moving it*) Now when you hold the bottle still and don't do anything to try to get rid of the glitter, what happens?

Bobby: It goes to the bottom.

Therapist: Is it very busy inside the bottle now, or is it pretty calm?

Bobby: It's pretty still and calm. *Therapist:* So the next time you feel very worried, and I know you have been worried about returning to school, could you be very still, like the bottle is now, and just notice whatever thoughts your mind is having, like you have been noticing the glitter in the bottle? Can you see now that the water is really still and it's very calm inside the bottle?

Bobby: Yeah, it's very different from when I was trying to move the glitter around in the bottle.

Therapist: Which way do you think is the best way to get the glitter to go to the bottom of the bottle—shaking it and turning it from side to side, or holding it still?

Bobby: Definitely holding it still; trying to move the glitter myself just makes it worse and moves it all around.

Therapist: Sometimes when we're really worried, trying to push away our worries can make them come back again. Instead, if we just notice what's happening in our mind, without trying to get rid of our worries, they can settle down, and sit in the back of our mind rather than racing around, just like the glitter settles in the bottle when we let it be.

Working with Bobby's Parents

Bobby's school was closed for two and a half months due to COVID-19. During that time, I saw Bobby twice. I spent about ten minutes at the end of each session giving his mom feedback (his father was at work), explaining what exercises we had done and why, including tasks for her to model to Bobby, and also asking her to encourage him to practice with her at home.

Before I started working with Bobby, his mom had previously always tried to come up with a way to help Bobby feel better, which often involved distraction (this is not a technique used in ACT, as it promotes avoidance of thoughts and feelings, rather than letting them be). As a result, I gave Bobby's mom guidance about how she could encourage him to let it be, and sit with his thoughts and feelings, without trying to do anything with them. I recommended that she remind Bobby that his thoughts and feelings can't harm him, as he had learned in his sessions with me.

I also suggested to Bobby's mom that she practice using the common *let it go* technique "I am having the thought that" (Hayes & Smith, 2005) and add words such as "I am not sure what to cook for dinner," and "My mind is telling me that I feel tired/hungry/etc." I recommended that she say these statements aloud, not only in front of Bobby, but also in front of her husband and their younger children, using neutral, everyday statements. This way Bobby would hopefully begin to start using this technique himself, as part of how he relates to and interacts with his own thoughts.

Having Bobby's mom practice and reinforce the ACT techniques with Bobby that are being used in his therapy sessions is more likely to help Bobby attain quicker and lasting results than if he is required to remember to use these techniques himself. Not only are Bobby's parents being trained in *how* they can use ACT with Bobby and their other children, but they are also trained in how to use ACT in the same *way* that I used ACT with Bobby. If parents can practice these techniques in front of their child and provide consistency between home and therapy, they are helping to reduce the possibility of the child being confused about what strategies are being recommended for them.

In addition to asking Bobby's mom to practice and model techniques for Bobby, I also provided Bobby's parents with the following recommendations for his return to school:

- When you drive Bobby to school on the first day, chat with him in the car like it's any other day.
- If he's anxious, gently reassure Bobby that it's okay to feel nervous/scared/worried, and that he can take those feelings to school with him: those feelings are normal, and there will be other children and teachers who feel the same as him.
- Let Bobby know that you feel nervous when you haven't been to work for a while, and that's okay: feeling nervous/scared/worried can't hurt him, he is safe at school, and nothing bad will happen to him.
- Tell Bobby that he *does* cope with change, even if he doesn't always think so: remind him that on a family holiday he chose to go on the diving boards at the swimming pool. Although he was really scared when he first saw them, he decided to have a go because he saw other people having fun, and he thought he would regret it later if he didn't try. (*You will remember that in chapter 2 we*

looked at the case conceptualization template. In my first session with Bobby, during the case conceptualization process, he informed me about having gone on diving boards at a swimming pool when I asked if he could think of another time when his mind had told him not to do something because he was sad/afraid/worried/etc., but he did it anyway. You can bring in examples from the case conceptualization process of choose what matters and do what matters that the child has told you about, to help them let it be.)

- When you arrive at school, if Bobby becomes teary, don't leave school with Bobby to drive around the surrounding streets. It's okay to pull over outside school or near school and spend some time reassuring him—tell Bobby he is his own superhero who can get himself through this.

- *Do not* offer to pick him up from school early. Reassure Bobby that he can let his thoughts and feelings be; they will not hurt him, and they won't be with him forever.

- Tell Bobby that he has everything he needs to get through the school day, because he has gotten himself through other situations when he felt worried.

- Remember that we don't want to teach Bobby that worries need to be feared and avoided, or that he has to leave a situation when he is feeling very worried.

- After school, tell him how proud you are of him for going to school, and remind him that he did it, by himself.

Bobby's mom emailed me on his first day back at school to say that she had dropped him off at school, and that he was happy and relaxed.

Suggestions for Parents

When providing parents with suggestions about how they can remind their child of *let it be* and *let it go* and reinforce these processes at home, I make sure to recommend simple, neutral examples that parents can use as part of their day-to-day activities. When the child hears their parents using language consistent with the ACT Kidflex processes, this may remind them of what they've learned in therapy sessions and increase their likelihood of incorporating ACT strategies into their own coping toolkit.

You can recommend to parents that they use some of the exercises you have done with their child in therapy sessions. For example, when cooking, the parent can say, "I don't think I'm doing a very good job cooking this new recipe; thanks mind for that thought, it's the most interesting thought I've had all day!" The parent can also sing their thoughts to the tune of a favorite song (they can try to choose a tune that their child is likely to recognize, which might be fun for the child to hear). They can also rephrase the thought to become the title of a story (for example, "Here's the story of I'm no good at cooking," or "Here's the terrible cook story"). Then, the parent can say the title like it's a voice-over in a movie, and invite the child to try saying some different voice-overs for the title of the parent's story, which might be enjoyable for both the parent and child.

Conclusion

In this therapy session, you have introduced the child to *let it be* and *let it go* and have given them some new ways to interact with their thoughts and feelings. These include some fun exercises, which are probably quite different from how the child has previously tried to manage their problem or difficulty. Doing these exercises in therapy sessions, together with home tasks to practice the new techniques, can strengthen and build on what the child learned in the previous session. The next chapter focuses on helping the child to identify what really matters to them, and actions they can do, in order to do what matters to them instead of avoiding things that are important to them.

CHAPTER 4

Choose What Matters and Do What Matters

We read in the previous chapter that it's often appropriate to begin therapy with children with *let it be* (letting unwanted private experiences just be there, without trying to do anything with them) and *let it go* (stepping back and getting some separation between us and our thoughts, so that we are not stuck or attached to them). After spending the second session addressing these two processes, it works well to focus on *choose what matters* (identifying things that are important to the child, for example, looking after their pet) and *do what matters* (using behaviors related to *choose what matters*, for example, playing in the yard with their pet, in order to ensure that their pet gets enough exercise) in the third session. In this chapter, we'll look at how to talk to children about *choose what matters* and *do what matters*, as well as how to do exercises geared toward these two processes in sessions.

If, through my case conceptualization, I identify a clear rationale for addressing *choose what matters* and *do what matters*, I ensure that when I introduce these two processes to the child, I make *very* clear the link between these processes and the reason they are seeing me. If you don't do this, and instead presume that the child will make the connection, they might not see how the discussions and exercises relate to them, and they may also wonder what the purpose of the exercises are. For example, let's say you are working with a child who experiences anxiety when they attend school trips to the zoo, museums, and other unfamiliar places. The child stops attending all school trips in response to feeling anxious. Although not attending school trips helps the child avoid experiencing anxiety, the child starts fearing trips to *all* unfamiliar places, including places their family wishes to visit and travel to. After the child's classmates return from school trips, they often talk excitedly about what fun they had, and the child feels left out, uncomfortable, and embarrassed that they didn't attend the trip. The child tells you that not going to unfamiliar places helps prevent them from feeling anxious (we call this strategy *avoidance*), but they don't enjoy feeling disconnected from their peers after their classmates return from trips. The child's use of avoidance is not consistent with the goal of the ACT Kidflex (*I am flexible*), so you could focus your work with the child on addressing what matters to them (in this case, feeling connected to their peers). You would follow this by helping them *do what matters* by visiting unfamiliar places, even when they feel anxious, in order to be able to go on school trips with their peers, without having to be free of anxiety in order to attend.

Introducing Choose What Matters and Do What Matters

As I mentioned earlier, there's no rule or consensus among therapists for which order the ACT processes should be addressed in. Some ACT therapists start therapy with values (*choose what matters*) and committed action (*do what matters*), while others address these processes in the last session. It's important that you be flexible about which process(es) you address, and when, based on what you feel the child needs to learn about most at that time. With this in mind, I usually find that addressing *choose what matters* and *do what matters* after *let it be* and *let it go* works well with children. This is because I will have already given the child tools to let their thoughts and feelings be, and then let go of them, which in most cases results in the child's feeling more able and ready to begin or resume doing things that are important to them.

By addressing *choose what matters* and *do what matters* closer to the start of therapy rather than at the end, the child also has the opportunity to discuss any difficulties they may encounter trying to do what matters. But if you don't address these processes until the final session, the child might only start trying to do what matters *after* finishing therapy, and not have an opportunity to discuss their experiences with you. It's important that the child be able to discuss any difficulties in order to make effective and lasting changes to how they cope. You might also only be able to see the child for a few sessions due to time constraints on your role (for example, if you work in a school, you might only be permitted to see each child for a few sessions), so addressing *choose what matters* and *do what matters* early may help you to assist the child quickly and effectively.

When you teach the child about *choose what matters* and *do what matters*, this sows the seeds for the child to begin taking back some of the power they have often been giving to their mind. When I introduce these two processes, I explain to the child that while they can't choose *what* thoughts their mind comes up with, they *do* have a choice about how much they allow their thoughts to boss them around and tell them what to do, and what not to do. You'll know the child is responding to this idea when they, their parent, or their teacher tells you that the child has started doing things they haven't done before or in a long time—for example, raising their hand in mathematics class to answer a question, even when they feel nervous that their answer might be incorrect, or volunteering to be the first person in class to present their project, even when their mind tells them that their project isn't very good.

By the time the child first comes to see you, they will probably have heard lots of strategies from well-meaning people about what they should do in order to cope with their problem or difficulty. When you introduce children to *choose what matters* and *do what matters*, it's very likely that you will be introducing them to a concept they haven't heard before—that if there's something that matters to them, the problem or difficulty doesn't need to stop them from doing things that matter. When you equip the child with the skills to choose what matters and do what matters, this very often brings a newfound sense of freedom and relief, which may have a positive impact on their self-esteem, particularly if they have felt very burdened or overwhelmed by their problem or difficulty.

When I introduce children to *choose what matters* and *do what matters,* they often respond very positively to hearing that they have some choice about how to deal with their problem or difficulty. When this occurs, I frequently observe changes in children's postures—from being slumped in their chair to sitting up straight and beaming at the suggestion of being able to choose and do what's important to them. I've also observed parents respond with animation and enthusiasm, as they turn to their child and say something like "That sounds great; would you like to try that?" That kind of response from the parent might also affirm for the child that they are capable of creating change themself. Once children have learned about *choose what matters* and *do what matters,* they often feel empowered to start making some changes to how they cope.

Let's look now at how you can explain *choose what matters* and *do what matters* to children as well as some questions you can ask to help children understand what these two processes are all about.

Helping Children Choose What Matters

When you talk to children about *choose what matters,* they might tell you what they think you *want* to hear, or what their parents and teachers have told them *ought* to matter to them. With this in mind, a helpful way of introducing choose what matters can be: "Try to put aside what the adults in your life tell you *should* matter to you—like what your parents and teachers say you should care about—and think about what *really* matters to you. Think about what's *really* in your heart, and what you care about most."

As with other processes, giving an example from your own life will facilitate the child's engagement in the discussion. After providing the child with an example of what matters, shift the discussion to what the child might be missing out on, which you can do by asking, "Are your thoughts and feelings stopping you from doing anything that matters to you?"

On the following page, you'll find a worksheet that you can invite the child to complete, which is available for download in color from http://www.newharbinger.com/49760.

Worksheet 3: Write a Thank You Card to Yourself

Think about one thing that you do that's really important to you, for example, taking care of your pet or being kind and caring to other people. Now write a thank you card to yourself, thanking yourself for doing that one thing. When you've finished, you can decorate the card.

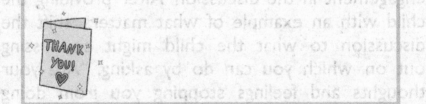

The next section outlines how you can use the magic wand question (see the case conceptualization template in chapter 2 for more detail) with the *choose what matters* process.

The Magic Wand Question

In chapter 2, we read that you can ask the child to pretend you have a magic wand, and it could allow them to start doing something they haven't done before that really matters to them, or start doing it more often.

Let's look at how the magic wand question might be used with a child with social anxiety disorder:

"Let's pretend that I had a magic wand. I wish I did, but I don't, as magic wands aren't real, but let's just pretend that I do. Imagine that it could help you cope with your thoughts and feelings, and you could start doing things, having to do with being around people, that you haven't done before and that really matter to you, or you could start doing these things more often. What could you start to do, or do more often?"

The child might reply that they would go to birthday parties, or family gatherings, or go to church with their family, or go the mall when it's full of people, or arrive at school on time in the mornings and walk into class with everyone else, instead of arriving late. Ask the child if they would like to choose one or two of these as goals to work toward in your sessions, letting them know that you would like to help them start to do something or several things that matter to them.

If you choose to ask the child the magic wand question, afterward you can invite the child to complete the following worksheet, which can be downloaded in color from http://www.newha rbinger.com/49760. To use this worksheet in sessions, I recommend offering the child a variety of materials to use, such as colored pencils, markers, or oil pastels. Also have available an assortment of things they can use to decorate the wand, such as heart-shaped, star-shaped, and rhinestone stickers in a variety of colors (these can usually be purchased at dollar stores), which often leads to greater engagement by the child in this exercise. Once the child has completed the worksheet, ask them if they would like to take it home. You might also want to suggest that they put it on their wall or elsewhere in their room where they can look at it. This may help the child start choosing what matters to them, as they will be reminded of what matters to them when they look at the worksheet. If the child doesn't want to complete the worksheet in the session, you can offer for them to take it home to complete. You might notice that while the case conceptualization template asks the child to imagine that the therapist has a magic wand, the worksheet asks the child to imagine that they have a magic wand. This is so that the worksheet can be used either in a therapy session or at home without the therapist present.

Worksheet 4: The Magic Wand

Magic wands aren't real, but let's pretend that you have a magic wand that could help you cope with your thoughts and feelings, and that you could start doing things that *really* matter to you, or you could do these things more often. Draw a magic wand, and write down some of the things you could start to do, or do more often.

When you've finished, you might like to decorate the magic wand.

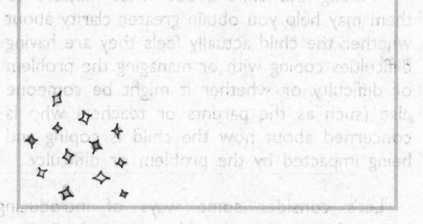

The Heart of Choose What Matters

Once the child has chosen what matters to them, ask what it is about those things that matters to them. I recommend letting the child know that you are not asking *why* those things matter, so they understand that you are not suggesting that those things *shouldn't* matter to them. For example, if a child doesn't attend parties and selects going to parties as something that matters, you could ask, "What is it about going to parties that is important to you?" (instead of asking "Why are parties important to you?"), and you could also ask, "What do you think you might miss out on when you choose not to go to a party?"

HELPFUL HINT

Asking the child about what matters to them may help you obtain greater clarity about whether the child actually feels they are having difficulties coping with or managing the problem or difficulty, or whether it might be someone else (such as the parents or teacher) who is concerned about how the child is coping and being impacted by the problem or difficulty.

Let's consider some ways of introducing *choose what matters* to a hypothetical client of yours named Daniel. Daniel is a seven-year-old boy who plays hockey in his community. His parents brought him to see you because he has been feeling depressed and lately has been refusing to go to hockey practice. Daniel told you that when he feels depressed, he doesn't try to do anything to get rid of or avoid these feelings. He also said that when he feels sad, he's certain he won't enjoy playing hockey, so he doesn't go to hockey practice—instead, he stays home. You addressed *let it be* and *let it go* the first time you met Daniel so that he would begin to feel less overpowered and controlled by his thoughts and feelings. In the second session, you address *choose what matters* because when Daniel feels sad, he stops doing things that matter to him, which makes his thoughts and feelings seem even stronger. You ask Daniel what it is about playing hockey and attending practice that matters to him, and what he might miss out on when he doesn't attend. Daniel shares that he usually has fun with his friends, enjoys being part of a team, and feels more energized after attending practice. You learn that Daniel is the goalkeeper, and his teammates cheer for him when he does a good job keeping the ball of out of the net, which leads to his feeling that he is a valued member of the team.

What are some approaches you could take at this point? You could encourage Daniel to attend hockey practice, even when his mind tells him that he feels sad and shouldn't go. You could also ask Daniel what might make it difficult to attend practice when he's sad, and what he might try to do in order to attend. Another approach is to ask him to think about whether there's something that his parents could do that might help him attend practice, especially when his mind tells him that he can't or doesn't want to go. For example, his parents could remind him that once he arrives, he really enjoys it, even when his mind tells him that he doesn't want to go (you'd want to purposely use the phrase "your mind tells you" to remind Daniel of the *let it go* process).

You could also give Daniel a sheet of paper and invite him to write some statements about what matters to him about playing hockey. When Daniel finishes writing, you could suggest that he put the sheet on the wall in his bedroom and look at it when he doesn't want to attend practice—as a reminder of what matters to him—then go to practice, even though his mind is having the thought that he doesn't want to go (this combines *choose what matters*, *do what matters*, and *let it go*).

There are many more *choose what matters* exercises you can use in sessions, including worksheets and art exercises, as well as suggestions you can give to parents for home tasks. We'll cover these next.

Choose What Matters Exercises

In chapter 3, we read about how art exercises can be used to teach children the *let it be* and *let it go* processes. I've found that art exercises are also a great way of introducing *choose what matters* to children. We will look now at art exercises for *choose what matters:*

Draw or Paint a Treasure Chest or Backpack (adapted from Coyne, 2011)

Invite the child to draw a treasure chest or backpack containing all the things that matter to them. Then you can invite the child to label these things next to the treasure chest or backpack. The child might also like to decorate the treasure chest or backpack.

Write a "Thank You For Being You" Card

Invite the child to think about what matters to them about themselves and imagine that a friend, family member, teacher, or coach is writing them a "thank you for being you" card. Then invite the child to write this card to themself. If the child is unsure what to write, you could give an example, such as a family member thanking them for being very helpful at home or a teacher thanking them for always volunteering to help out (for example, by collecting notices from the school office). Once the child has written the card, they might like to decorate it.

Note: If the child has completed Worksheet 3, don't suggest this exercise as it would be too repetitive.

Write a Birthday Card to Yourself

Invite the child to write a birthday card to themself and include all of the things that matter to them about themself, then decorate it like a birthday card.

Write an Elementary School Graduation Card

Invite the child to write a card to themself for graduating from elementary school, writing about all the things they do that are important to them (for example, being kind and caring to others or taking care of their pet), and then invite them to decorate it like a graduation card.

Draw or Paint a Heart

Invite the child to draw or paint a heart and then write the things that matter to them inside the heart. (If the child chooses to use paint, I recommend offering them cut-up strips of paper to write the statements on, and have them stick the statements on top of the paint, instead of waiting for the paint to dry and then trying to write statements on the paint.)

Let's look now at an example of how you could use one of these art exercises in a session with another hypothetical client. Sarah is six-year-old girl whose uncle passed away a few weeks ago. This was the first time anyone close to her had passed away. Her parents brought Sarah to you for therapy because she has avoided visiting her aunt and cousins since his passing. Sarah misses them, particularly her cousins, and wants to visit them, but she feels sad, nervous, and uncomfortable about going there now, particularly because he passed away at home. Sarah loves her aunt and cousins and worries about them, but she's confused about whether to visit them. You decide to introduce *choose what matters* to Sarah to help her connect with what is important to her about her aunt and cousins.

Let's consider how you might approach it from here. You could ask Sarah why she likes spending time with her relatives (rather than asking "what matters" to her about spending time with her relatives, which she might not understand) and what she might miss out on by avoiding going to their home. You might learn, for example, that she usually enjoys playing with her cousins and their cat and watching their fish swim in the tank. Or she might reveal that her aunt and cousins fuss over her, and whenever she spends time with them, she feels very connected to them and tells her cousins that she wishes they were her sisters. You could then encourage Sarah to visit them, even when her mind tells her that she feels sad and nervous about going to their house.

You know that Sarah loves drawing, so you might give her a sheet of paper and invite her to draw a heart. Then you could suggest that inside the heart, she write down why she likes spending time with her relatives (or you could write the statements for her if she has difficulty writing or spelling). When Sarah is finished, you could ask her if she would like to take her drawing home to remind her of why she likes visiting her aunt and cousins.

Now that we've looked at *choose what matters*, let's look at how to introduce the child to *do what matters*.

Helping Children Do What Matters

After you have helped the child identify what matters to them, you can help the child come up with some specific actions they can start doing, based on what matters to them. I suggest spending some time discussing *how* they will put what matters to them into action: this will help you and the child come up with specific actions. For example, the child might say that they worry about their homework, which they find difficult, and that doing well in school is important to them. An action they could start doing is asking their teacher for help when they are unable to complete their homework, which is based on wanting to do well in school.

In addition to exercises the child does in therapy sessions, *do what matters* includes actions such as attending therapy sessions, completing home tasks that you recommend to the child, and starting to do things that matter to them, based on *choose what matters*. Kirk Strosahl (2015) suggested that when addressing *do what matters*, it's essential to help the client develop a realistic and achievable plan so that they are more likely to experience success than failure.

Asking the child the following question will help the two of you develop a workable plan for *do what matters*: "What are some *small* things you can start doing that matter to you?" For example, a child tells you that they want to make more friends or new friends at school but hasn't tried to get to know many children because they are worried that children won't want to play with or talk to them. They also think that most people don't like them once they get to know them. You might suggest that the child begin by approaching another child who is also sitting alone at lunch and invite them to sit with them or play in the playground together.

A very effective way for helping children do what matters is using role-play during sessions. Using the above example of the child who wants to make more or new friends, you could invite the child to take part in a role-play with you where you pretend to be the client, and the client pretends to be another child at school. In the role-play, the child approaches you and invites you to sit with them at lunch or play in the playground together. You can encourage the child to notice how they feel in their body, letting these feelings and sensations be without trying to do anything with them (this reminds the child of *let it be*) while continuing to take part in the role-play. After the role-play is finished, ask the child how they felt in their body and what the experience of approaching you as a pretend child at school and inviting you to join them was like. Then, ask the child if they think they could approach a child at school, starting with once or twice during the coming week. If the child replies that they are going to do this every day, I recommend suggesting that they start slowly, aiming for once or twice a week instead. This is more likely to be achievable and sustainable over time (whereas trying to do this every day might lead the child to give up completely after a short time because it feels too stressful or overwhelming).

When addressing *do what matters* challenges, the aim is to explore what factors might get in the way of the child's following through on the actions that are in line with what matters to them. A direct approach is to ask the child, "Is there anything that might make it difficult for you to do this?" If the child says yes, you could ask for more information, and then ask, "What could you do that might help you to do these things?"

For example, you could suggest to the child that it might be difficult to decide at lunch whom to approach, and ask if they might be willing to discuss whom to approach with their parent at home the night before. You could also suggest choosing a few children to approach in case they are unable to find one of them. You might also encourage the child to practice role-playing with someone in their family in order to gain more confidence for approaching children at school. This may also help them remember what they would like to say and could increase the child's willingness to do this task.

Just as we saw in chapter 3 that *let it be* and *let it go* are complementary, so too are *choose what matters* and *do what matters*. So let's look at how we combine these two processes.

Exercises Combining Choose What Matters and Do What Matters

In this section you'll learn exercises and techniques you can use with children to combine choose *what matters* and *do what matters,* using case examples to illustrate most of these activities.

What's in My Heart

For children aged five to eight years, an approach that works really well is to start with the *choose what matters* activity of draw or paint a heart, and then ask the child to choose one thing that matters most to them or that's most important to them. I recommend that you give the child an example of something that matters, like the following: "For example, if spending time with your younger sibling on the weekend matters to you, you could ask them to play a game or ball with you, or do an art project together."

After the child has thought of something that matters to them, they can write this inside the heart (or you can offer to write it for them if they have difficulties writing). Then ask them to think of one action they could do that relates to what matters to them, and they can write this inside the heart (or outside if there's insufficient room). Once the child has thought of an action, ask if there is anything they might need to do first in order to do that action. For example, if they choose to do an art exercise, they might need to ask their parent what a suitable art exercise might be, to ensure that it's age-appropriate for their younger sibling, and when it would be suitable to do the exercise.

For children aged nine to twelve years, I developed a more complex version of this exercise, which is *generally* suitable for children this age, but use your judgment and knowledge of the child to determine whether it's appropriate for them. If you think the exercise is too complex, you can use the simpler exercise for children aged five to eight years described above. I adapted this exercise from Dahl and Lundgren's (2006) Bull's-Eye.

For the first step, give the child a piece of paper and a choice of markers or pencils, and invite them to draw a heart. Then ask the child to choose one thing that matters most to them (*choose what matters*), and write that in the middle of the heart. You can use the earlier example, explaining that if spending time with their sibling is something that matters, they could write that. Next, ask the child to think about whether they actually *do* the thing that matters—for example, spend time with their sibling.

The next step is to invite the child to draw a dot inside the heart, to show how close or how far away they are from doing what matters (for example, spending time with their sibling). You can explain that if they feel that they *do* spend a lot of time with their sibling, then they could draw a dot close to the middle of the heart, but if they feel that they *don't* spend much time with their sibling, then they could draw the dot farther away. I recommend that you explain to the child that you are asking about whether they actually *do* the thing that matters to them, and if so, it might help to think about how often they spend time doing this.

After the child has drawn the dot in the heart, ask them if there's anything that might make it difficult to do that action (such as spending time with their sibling), and what actions they might be able to do (*do what matters*) to help them move closer to what matters to them. You might like to give the child an example (such as inviting their sibling to play a game); then you could ask them to come up with some actions of their own, which you could suggest they write outside the heart. Last, ask the child, "What might make it difficult to do these actions regularly?"

In my experience, not only does the What's in My Heart exercise help children think about what matters to them, but it also helps them see how close or far away they are from what matters to them. Like the Magic Wand worksheet we saw earlier in this chapter, this exercise creates a nice visual for children, and they may like to take their drawing home to put on the wall in their bedroom.

Two Roads

When I was a teenager, I remember my mom saying that in most situations people have two choices—going down one road leads to one outcome, and going down another road leads to a different outcome. She talked about her own childhood, and said that even if you grew up seeing your parents doing things a certain way, you have a choice when you're older about whether to copy these behaviors or do things differently. With my mom's words in mind, I developed the Two Roads exercise to combine *choose what matters* and *do what matters*. The exercise helps children see where *not doing* what matters to them can lead to, and where *doing* what matters to them can lead to. I find that this exercise not only helps children understand these two processes, but also helps make these processes very relevant for the child. I also find that it works well for both online and face-to-face sessions. In short, the exercise involves (1) having the child write down something that matters most to them (*choose what matters*); (2) drawing two roads; and (3) having the child list beside one road the things that take them away from doing that thing that matters most to them, and beside the other road the things that takes them close to doing that thing. I'll explain the exercise in more detail below.

Let's look now at two case examples that combine *choose what matters* and *do what matters* activities.

Case Example: Zahara, Eleven Years Old

Zahara's mother contacted me after Zahara was pressured by her peers to engage in an inappropriate activity she didn't wish to be part of. Because this was during COVID-19, all of our sessions were conducted online. At her mother's request, I met with her mother for a few minutes before seeing Zahara. Her mother described Zahara as someone who needs to be liked, and said she wanted Zahara to feel more confident, so she could walk away from situations where she felt uncomfortable, instead of giving in to peer pressure. I saw Zahara on three occasions.

The following transcript shows how I introduced *choose what matters* to Zahara.

Therapist: Zahara, if I could help you to start doing some things that matter to you, what would you be doing?

Zahara: Well, something happened with kids at school; I said no, but felt pressured to join in. I want to know how to handle things, and not give in to other people. I want to be able to stand up for myself, and walk away from my friends if there are problems in the group that I haven't caused. My mom tells me that I'm too nice, because even though I say no to people, I end up saying yes.

Therapist: How do you want to be when you are with other people, and what's important to you about how you behave when you are with your friends?

Zahara: I want to be smart, caring, kind, friendly, brave, not afraid to be myself, and have the courage to say no when I know something isn't right or doesn't feel right. I want to stand up for myself and for what's right, and not follow others when they are mean to other people.

Therapist: There are a lot of great things that matter to you. Which of these are most important to you? Perhaps you could try to choose one that matters the most, or you can choose a few.

Zahara: It is definitely having the courage to say no when I know something isn't right, not being afraid to be myself, and being able to stand up for myself.

Therapist: Now I would like to invite you to think about how you *don't* want to be when you are with your friends. What sorts of behaviors *don't* you want to do?

Zahara: I don't want to be mean, or bossy. But I also don't want to be *too* nice, and always say yes to people, instead of standing up for what's right. I also don't want to tell other people to do things they don't want to do.

After hearing from Zahara what mattered to her, I decided to do the Two Roads exercise so she could see how *choose what matters* relates to *do what matters.*

Using the Two Roads Exercise with Zahara

I asked Zahara to get a piece of paper and a pen or pencil, and I invited her to think about what matters most to her about how she wants to behave when she spends time with other people, including her friends. I asked her to try to come up with one sentence to describe that, and write it at the top of the page. Zahara wrote, "Being myself, instead of pretending to be very confident or very funny." I asked Zahara to draw two roads, leaving room in between the roads for writing, and label the first road as "Road A" and the second as "Road B." Then I asked Zahara to write the heading "How I *don't* want to be with my friends" to the left of Road A, followed by "How I *do* want to be with my friends" to the left of Road B.

I invited Zahara to write all the actions next to Road A that would take her *away* from how she wants to be with others (for example, copying her friends when they are mean to other girls at school). Next to Road B, I invited Zahara to list all the actions that would take her closer to how she *does* want to be when she's with others (for example, defending people when her friends speak badly about them behind their backs, and telling her friends that it's not nice to speak badly about others).

After Zahara finished listing all of the actions next to the two roads, I asked her to think about the following questions:

- "What are some things you could do if you notice you are doing things on Road A (how you *don't* want to be, such as speaking badly about others behind their backs)?"
- "What are some things that might *help* you stay on Road B (how you *do* want to be, such as walking away when friends speak badly about others, or telling your friends that it's not nice to speak badly about others)?"

You'll notice that when I asked Zahara these questions, I used statements she had already given me about how she does and doesn't want to be with others. I did this to remind Zahara of what each road is, and I found that using the actions she had already come up with made it very clear for her what Road A and Road B were.

The Two Roads exercise worked really well online; Zahara was able to understand all the tasks and was very enthusiastic and engaged. When we finished, she stated that she found the exercise very helpful. If you are going to do this exercise online, I recommend that you contact the child's parent before the session and ask them to have some paper and pens, markers, or pencils ready for the child to use in the session. Once the exercise is finished, you could ask the child to take a photo of their drawing with their phone and ask their parent to email it to you, so you have a copy for their file. If the child doesn't have a phone of their own, you could ask if they are comfortable asking their parent (where appropriate) to photograph the drawing and to email it to you. This exercise would also work well in face-to-face sessions.

Now I'd like to introduce you to another child with whom I also combined *choose what matters* and *do what matters* in the same session. First, I'll provide a detailed description of what occurred in the first two sessions and why I addressed *let it be, choose what matters*, and *do what matters* in the second session (rather than waiting until the third session to introduce the latter two processes), followed by a transcript of the second session.

Case Example: Belinda, Eight Years Old

Belinda has obsessive compulsive disorder and turns the faucet on and off repeatedly in multiples of four. She fears if she doesn't do this, something bad will happen. The first session with Belinda and her mother was spent developing a case conceptualization, which was fairly brief, as her difficulties had only begun a few months prior, following her aunt's passing and her uncle being diagnosed with cancer. After completing the case conceptualization, we still had time remaining before the session finished, so I introduced a discussion about *let it be* (see chapter 3 for more detail).

At the start of our second session, Belinda and her mother told me that Belinda was still turning the faucet on and off repeatedly, and she had also stopped leaving the house, except to attend school (which had just finished for the six-week summer vacation), because she was afraid something bad would happen. It was my last day at work before my own summer vacation commenced, and I knew that I wouldn't be seeing Belinda again for another six weeks. Upon hearing that Belinda didn't intend to leave the house for the next six weeks, I decided to skip *let it go* and continue addressing *let it be*, as well as introduce *choose what matters* and *do what matters*. I was concerned that if Belinda didn't leave the house for the next six weeks, returning to school after vacation might be really hard for her, and she might develop school refusal. I thought that continuing to focus on letting it be and teaching Belinda to choose what matters and do what matters might be the quickest and most powerful way to help her leave her home.

Before addressing *choose what matters* and *do what matters,* I invited Belinda to do an exercise with me as part of teaching her about *let it be,* using exposure response prevention (ERP) therapy (Hofmann & Smits, 2008) in combination with ACT. ERP involves having the child do things they are fearful of, or struggle with, in a safe way in therapy sessions. I felt that ERP might be very helpful because it is the most effective treatment for obsessive compulsive disorder, and ACT combined with ERP is as effective as ERP alone (Twohig et al., 2018).

You might feel anxious or worried at the suggestion of doing ERP with children, which, I want to reassure you, is really common, especially when it's your first time using it. The first time I used it, I know I was worried that I'd get it wrong and that the child would refuse to participate. You might also be unsure how to use ERP together with ACT. I recommend that if you are going to suggest to children (and their parents) that you use ERP, you let the child know that ERP has been found to be really helpful for children, teenagers, and adults, which might be reassuring for the child (and their parent).

Let's look now at how I combined ACT—focusing on *let it be*—with ERP with Belinda.

Using ACT and ERP with Belinda

I explained to Belinda and her mother that when people are fearful of things, it's often very helpful in therapy sessions to have them safely do the things they fear. Likewise, when children have thoughts that they have to do certain things, like turning the faucet on and off multiple times, it can be very helpful in sessions to spend some time together doing what they fear. I explained that this is called exposure response prevention, which can be shortened to ERP. I suggested to Belinda and her mother that we try ERP by going into the washroom in the clinic, and seeing what turning the faucet on would be like for Belinda.

As soon as I suggested this, Belinda jumped up from her seat and said that she'd like to try it. Her mother seemed very pleased with Belinda's enthusiastic response, and also agreed. The three of us went into the washroom, and I asked Belinda to just notice (*let it be*) how she was feeling in her body as we stood facing the sink. Belinda replied that she felt okay. Then I asked her if she would be willing to turn the faucet on and then turn it off, without turning it on and off again. She agreed, and was able to complete this. While we stood by the sink, I asked Belinda to again notice how she was feeling in her body *(let it be)* and what thoughts her mind was having (this introduces Belinda to *let it go*). She replied that she felt fine, but her mind was telling her to turn the faucet on again (Belinda has started using *let it go* herself).

As we stood watching the faucet, I asked Belinda to imagine a scale from 1 to 10, where 1 was not at all strong, and 10 was very strong, and to rate how strong the thought of wanting to turn the faucet on again was. Belinda rated it as 7. I encouraged her to just notice the thought *(let it be)* and walk away from the sink, then leave the washroom and return to the therapy room, which she did. Once we returned to the therapy room and were seated, I asked Belinda to again rate how strong the feeling of wanting to turn the faucet on again was, letting her know that it was okay if she rated the feeling the same as when we were in the washroom. (I did this so Belinda would know that she didn't have to try to please me by rating the feeling as lower this time.) Belinda rated the feeling as a 4.

You will recall that Belinda had also stopped going out, except to attend school, due to worrying that something bad would happen if she left the house. It was important to help Belinda identify what mattered to her about leaving the house *(choose what matters)* and to try to teach her that she can do the things that matter to her (do what matters), even if the thought about something bad happening shows up. With these ideas in mind, let's look now at a transcript of the second part of the session with Belinda, which focuses on the discussion we had in the therapy room after returning from the washroom.

Therapist: Belinda, last time we met you told me that you worry about something bad happening, and that you have been doing certain things when this thought shows up.

Belinda: Yes, I turn the faucet on and off a few times before I wash my hands or take a shower, or fill my water bottle or cup with water, always in multiples of four.

Therapist: Can you think of a time when you didn't do this, even if your mind told you to?

Belinda: At the beginning of the year before COVID-19, I didn't listen to my mind, but lately when my mind tells me to do it, I do; otherwise something bad will happen.

Therapist: And when you didn't listen to your mind (this teaches let it go), and didn't turn the faucet on and off several times, what happened?

Belinda: The thoughts actually stopped for a couple of months.

Therapist: And what happened when the thoughts started again?

Belinda: Since the thoughts came back, whenever I need to wash or get a drink of water, I've been turning the faucet on and off in multiples of four; otherwise I think something bad will happen.

Therapist: Do you think that turning the tap on and off in multiples of four has taken anything away from you—like if you weren't doing this, would you be doing something else with your time?

Belinda: Definitely! Sometimes I turn the faucet on and off forty times before I can walk away! Also worrying takes up a lot of time, because I worry about people like my friends and teachers finding out that I have to turn the faucet on and off, especially when I use the washroom at school or fill up my water bottle in the playground.

Therapist: What do you think your life would be like if you didn't do everything your mind told you to do?

Belinda: I wouldn't be stressed and angry. It would be like I wouldn't be stuck—I'd have more energy, and be calmer and free.

Therapist: And is there anything you've been missing out on, or anywhere you've stopped going, because of how you've been trying to deal with these thoughts?

Belinda: My friends have been inviting me to their houses, and to go out with them, like to the movies or the mall, but I've been saying no each time. Also, my parents, brother, and I used to go to my grandparents' house for lunch on Sundays, but I don't go anymore, because I feel safer at home. If I was to go out, I know that I'd spend the whole time worrying that something bad was going to happen, like I'll get sick, or that we will be in a car crash, or that something will happen to our house while we're out.

Therapist: Before these worries were happening, did you go out with friends, or to their houses?

What was it like going to those places, and to your grandparents' house?

Belinda: I loved it. I have fun at my friends' houses, and my best friend has a new puppy that I want to meet. I also really like going to my grandparents' house because they have chickens, and I get to collect the eggs. They also have a big vegetable garden, and I pick vegetables with my grandparents to take home.

Therapist: Wow, it sounds like doing these things are really important to you.

Belinda: They are.

Therapist: Can you tell me what it is about seeing your friends and visiting your grandparents that matters most to you? If that's hard to answer, can you think about what it is about seeing your friends and visiting your grandparents that's important to you?

Belinda: I have fun with my friends, and then at school on Mondays we talk about what we did together on the weekend. When I visit my grandparents, they teach me how to bake, or we do puzzles together, and they always have yummy chocolates and cookies.

Therapist: It sounds like you get to have some very special time with your friends and grandparents when you visit them. Let me ask you a question: how much power do you think your mind has over you? Does it just have a *little* power, so that you get to choose how much you listen to your mind, or do you think that your mind has *lots* of power—does it boss you around a lot and tell you what to do and what not to do?

Belinda: It *definitely* has lots of power over me: I do whatever it tells me to do.

Therapist: I have an idea, but first I just want to let you know that it might sound a little strange. That's because it's *quite* different from what you have been doing to manage this worry about something bad happening. We just saw in the washroom that even when your mind tells you to turn the faucet on and off multiple times, you don't have to do everything your mind tells you *(this teaches Belinda to let it go)*. I also want to suggest that you can do the things that matter to you, like visiting your friends, and meeting your best friend's new puppy, and visiting your grandparents, even when your mind tells you that something bad will happen. You don't need to try to do anything to get rid of the worry; you can actually take it with you (*let it be*).

Belinda: (laughs)

Therapist: I know that it sounds a bit strange! But if those things really matter to you, your worries don't have to stop you from doing those things.

Belinda: How would this work? How do I take my worries with me?

Therapist: When you go to your friends' houses, or you go to the mall with them, how do you usually get there?

Belinda: My parents usually drive me.

Therapist: And when do the worries start to show up?

Belinda: Usually right before we leave home, then we have to call and cancel and make up an excuse not to go.

Therapist: What do you think it would be like if when you are at home before going out, and you notice your worries showing up, instead of calling your friends and canceling, or getting your parents to call and cancel, you could try saying to yourself, "Come on worries *(this teaches Belinda to let it go)*, let's get in the car *(this teaches Belinda to let it be)*, it's time to go out now"? And when you get into the car, you can make space next to you on the seat for your worries *(let it be)*, and imagine that they are sitting next to you *(let it go)*. They can go with you to your friends' and grandparents' houses, and to the mall with you, instead of your worries having so much power of you and stopping you from going out.

Belinda: It sounds so different from what I do, but I'd like to try it.

Therapist: Is there anything that might make it hard to do these things?

Belinda: I guess it will feel a little weird at first, but I'd like to have a go at trying it.

Therapist: Belinda, you've done extremely well speaking about your thoughts and feelings, and trying some new things today. It's really great that you're willing to try some different ways of managing these worries.

Working with Belinda's Parent

At the end of each session with Belinda, I spent time giving her mom suggestions for how she could help Belinda practice what she had learned. Before I started working with Belinda, her mom had encouraged her to try to distract herself when she had thoughts that she had to turn the faucet on multiple times. Belinda and her mom both acknowledged that distraction wasn't helpful for Belinda, and, as we saw in chapter 3, distraction promotes avoidance of thoughts and feelings, rather than letting them be, so it's not used in ACT. Instead, I encouraged Belinda's mom to try to remind Belinda to let her thoughts be and let them go, by saying her own worries (appropriate for disclosure to her children) aloud in front of Belinda (and the rest of the family), such as, "Come on worries *(let it go)* about learning the new computer program at work, it's time to go to work now" *(let it be)*, and "When I get to work, I'm going to imagine that my worries about learning the new computer program are sitting next to me" *(let it go).*

HELPFUL HINT

Teaching parents how to remind their child of the ACT Kidflex processes using everyday situations enables them to reinforce what the child has learned in therapy sessions. This may

> help the child use the processes and develop better coping strategies.

To help Belinda connect with what matters to her, I recommended that Belinda's mom ask Belinda what matters to her about visiting her grandparents and reminding her how much she enjoys going to their home. Then I suggested that she encourage Belinda to come with the family to visit her grandparents, even if her mind tells her that she's afraid to, because her grandparents are important to her and she always has fun with them (*do what matters*).

I also suggested that after Belinda resumes visiting her grandparents, the next goal could be for Belinda to resume making arrangements with her friends. I recommended that Belinda's mom help Belinda do this by asking her what matters to her about having playdates with friends (*choose what matters*). I also suggested she remind Belinda of the reasons she enjoys going out with them and to their houses and that she encourage her to make arrangements (*do what matters*), even if her mind is telling her that she's worried. (This also reminds Belinda of *let it be* and *let it go*.)

Belinda visited her grandparents' home the day after the session where I addressed visiting her grandparents. Her mother informed me that the visit was very successful and that Belinda coped really well. Her mother also said that on the way to Belinda's grandparents' home, Belinda informed her mom that when she had gotten into the car, she had said to herself, *Sit down worries, we're off to visit grandma and grandpa.* Belinda's mom also let me know that Belinda hadn't been turning the faucet on and off repeatedly since our session, and that Belinda had also made arrangements to go to the park with her friends.

Now that we've seen an example of how to combine *choose what matters* and *do what matters* in therapy sessions, let's consider how to link the processes of the ACT Kidflex to each other and to the exercises the child has done.

Linking the ACT Kidflex Processes

In the above transcript of the second session, I asked Belinda some questions from the case conceptualization template (which we covered in chapter 2) about *let it be, choose what matters,* and *do what matters.* I made the links between the processes very clear so Belinda could see how they relate to each other and learn how to use them together.

It's important to explain to the child how *choose what matters* and *do what matters* relate to the exercises you and the child did together in the previous session(s). When the child can see *why* you're teaching them about something, they might be more likely to adopt the strategies in their day-to-day life and practice the exercises on their own. When you give feedback to the child's parents (where appropriate), you can also highlight how *choose what matters* and *do what matters* exercises relate to those used in the previous session(s), as you did with the child. I recommend that where possible, you do this for each process.

You can also create links when you suggest home tasks to the child (and their parent where appropriate) by reminding them of exercises they did in previous sessions and explaining how they can use the processes together, instead of separately. I often do this by telling the child (and their parent, where appropriate) that what we are doing in therapy is like building a toolkit for how to cope with or manage problems or difficulties, and that each tool is important, with no tool any more important than the others. Sometimes they might use several tools at a time that they learned in our sessions, while at other times they might use only one or two tools, and that's okay too.

HELPFUL HINT

If you don't make the links between the ACT Kidflex processes clear, and instead address each process separately, without connecting the exercises to those used in previous sessions, ACT can look clunky, as though it consists of separate, unrelated processes. Please be assured that it's very common for ACT to look clunky, especially when you're new to ACT. The more you use ACT, and practice it with your clients and in your own life, the smoother ACT with feel, and the more ways you'll find to connect the processes for your clients.

Ending Choose What Matters and Do What Matters Sessions

You've addressed *choose what matters* and *do what matters* with the child, and the end of the session is approaching. Let's look at some effective strategies for ending the session.

You can summarize the session by asking the child the following questions:

1. "Out of everything we've talked about today that matters to you, what is the *one* thing that matters the most?"

2. "Thinking about that one thing, what are some small things you can start to do toward that?" (You can name what the child identified as mattering the most.) If the child isn't sure what they could do, you could give them an example related to what they identified, such as, "If making some friends is what matters to you, perhaps you could ask your parents if you can invite someone

from school to your house on the weekend, or to go to the park or mall with you?"

3. "Is there anything that might make it hard or get in the way of you doing this?"

If the child identifies potential difficulties, you can break the task down, creating more manageable steps that they can do. For example, you could suggest that the child look through a class list with their parent to try to identify a child they might be comfortable trying to make plans with, and then you could suggest that the child role-play with you or their parent to practice inviting someone to their home. If all the steps that you suggest are met with resistance from the child, I recommend asking the child to come up with a different small step they could do, for example, asking a child at school to play ball with them at recess. Doing this smaller step first might empower the child to try a bolder step, like inviting someone for a playdate on the weekend.

HELPFUL HINT

Ensure that the child identifies small, realistic things they can do, to ensure a greater likelihood that they will be able to follow through and do something that matters to them. Otherwise, if the child elects to do something that's too bold, or too difficult, and they are unable to follow through with it, they might give up and think that they can't do things that really matter to them.

Before wrapping up this chapter, let's look at suggestions for *choose what matters* and *do what matters* that you can give to parents at the end of the child's session.

Suggestions for Parents

To help reinforce what their child has learned about *choose what matters* and *do what matters*, I recommend to parents that they invite the child to brainstorm *why* they identified particular things as important, and to think of an action they could do relating to what they identified as important. For example, if the child wants to make some new friends, you can suggest that the parent asks the child, "What is it about making some new friends that matters to you?" After the child has shared some reasons, the parent can ask the child, "What are some actions you could do to try to make new friends?" If the child doesn't feel comfortable sharing their reasons, the parents can let them know that's okay, and they can still ask the child to think of some actions to try to make new friends.

You can also let the parent know that they might need to help the child by suggesting some things the child could do (such as approaching some different children at recess or inviting some children for playdates on weekends). They could offer to help their child practice their skills for approaching new children by role-playing together at home, and if the parent drives the child to school, they could also offer to role-play with the child in the car, which might help the child remember what to say once they are at school.

Conclusion

In this session, you have introduced the child to *choose what matters* and *do what matters,* and they have learned that they don't have to avoid places or situations that matter to them just because of their thoughts and feelings. The child is likely to be empowered by this session and may feel that they now have a choice about how much they listen to their mind and how much power their problem or difficulty has over them. The exercises in this session may have shown the child how they can start choosing what matters and start doing things that matter to them, using some small, realistic, and achievable steps. These skills have built on what the child learned in the previous session, which may have focused on *let it be* and *let it go.* Or, you might have introduced the child to *choose what matters* and *do what matters* after the first session, instead of after introducing *let it be* and *let it go,* depending on what the child needed most. In the next chapter, we'll look at how you can teach children to stay in the present; be aware of what's happening around them, rather than being caught up in their thoughts and feelings; and notice themselves, in order to give them greater insight about the impact of their actions.

CHAPTER 5

Stay Here and Notice Yourself

Now that you've addressed *let it be* and *let it go*, and *choose what matters* and *do what matters*, it's time to address the final two processes of the ACT Kidflex. These are *stay here* (being present and aware of your experiences, such as listening to a song and hearing all of the sounds, instruments, and words) and *notice yourself* (standing back and watching yourself, such as stopping when you're shouting at your sibling, and noticing that you feel very angry that they wore your favorite sweater without asking your permission). In this chapter, we'll look at how to introduce these two processes to children, use *stay here* and *notice yourself* exercises in sessions, and recommend exercises to children and their parents for practice at home.

Introducing Stay Here

When introducing *stay here* to children, I usually start by asking if they have heard the term "mindfulness" before. Most children have: often they've done programs at school focused on calming the mind, and they might reply with something like "You're talking about meditation; I do that at school," or they may tell you that they use an application on their phone to help relax before going to sleep. In this case, I say something like "Meditation is one way of staying here, and trying to keep our minds present on what's happening, but there are several others, and I'd like to introduce you to some exercises that other children I have worked with have found helpful."

When I am explaining *stay here* to children, I describe it as *really* noticing what's happening right now inside your body and around you: really being in the moment instead of only focusing on your thoughts. To help the child understand the concept of *stay here*, I often ask, "Have you ever had the experience where someone is talking to you, and you realize that even though you have been standing right next to them, looking in their eyes while they are talking to you, you were actually thinking about something else, so afterward you don't remember anything they said?" Most children answer yes to this question!

Another example that I use with older children (around eight to twelve years old), who are likely to be reading independently, is "Have you ever noticed when you are reading a book, that you get to the bottom of the page and realize that you don't remember anything you read?" If the child replies yes, you can reply that this happens to a lot of people, including yourself!

This is often a good opportunity to have a discussion with the child about situations where we are able to stay here, and situations where our minds are elsewhere.

Let's look now at an exercise you can use to continue this discussion with children.

Staying Here and Being Elsewhere

I developed this exercise with Louise Hayes for my Doctor of Philosophy degree (Black, 2016). I have done this exercise with children during online sessions where I used a digital whiteboard, and I've also done it in face-to-face sessions using paper. For this exercise, draw a vertical line down the middle of the whiteboard or paper to create two columns. Write the heading "Staying Here" at the top of the first column, and "Being Elsewhere" at the top of the second column. I recommend that you begin the exercise by sharing a neutral example of your own for each column. For example, you might say that cooking is a time when you stay here, while standing in line at the bank or post office is a time when you are generally elsewhere. After you have given the child examples, ask them to think of some examples of their own for each column. If the child is unsure, you could ask them about their experience in very specific situations, for example, eating breakfast, sitting in class, playing a musical instrument, attending swimming lessons, doing chores, listening to their favorite song, and doing crafts or puzzles. Write the child's responses on the whiteboard or paper, and then invite the child to come up with some examples of their own for both columns (or you can do the writing if the child prefers). For each example, ask the child if they feel that they stay here in that situation, or whether they feel that they are elsewhere. Then you could ask the child the following questions:

- "What makes it hard to stay here?"
- "What situations could you try to practice staying here?"
- "What small step(s) could you start to do, to try to stay here?"

Once you have introduced the child to the concept of staying here and being elsewhere, use experiential exercises to teach the child the *stay here* process. We'll look at some of these exercises below.

Stay Here Exercises

I recommend that you choose one *stay here* exercise from the selection of experiential exercises below to do with the child in the session. In my experience, it's often more powerful to do one experiential exercise per session instead of several, as the child will be more likely to remember the exercise after the session, and then be able to practice it on their own at home or school if they wish to. However, if you finish an experiential exercise quickly, or the child is not engaged in the exercise (they might seem disinterested or ask you if they can do something else), then you might wish to try a different experiential exercise. For each of the following exercises, I'll suggest some instructions, but feel free to modify these exercises.

Eating While Staying Here

For this exercise, it's important to always check with the child's parent in advance whether they consent to you doing this exercise with the child during the next session. If the parent consents, I recommend asking the parent to bring something for the child to eat during the next session, and giving the parents an example of a food that's suitable for this exercise, such as dried or fresh fruit, vegetable sticks, or a small candy bar.

Invite the child to take part in this exercise, letting them know that in a moment, you will ask them to pick up the food they have brought from home, and then you will give them instructions, which you would like them to listen to carefully before eating the food. The reason I suggest giving these instructions first is that I've had the experience where chocolate or candy has been used for this exercise, and the child has eaten it before I've finished giving them instructions about what we're going to do!

The following script was written by Amy Saltzman and Philippe Goldin (Saltzman & Goldin, 2008, p.147) for eating while staying here. You can download this script at http://www.newharbinger.com/49760, but remember, you don't have to use an exact script; you can make up your own.

Take one bite, paying attention to what is happening in your mouth, noticing the taste. Don't rush; take one bite at a time, noting how the taste changes, how your teeth and tongue work ... See if you can notice the urge to swallow, and then feel the swallow as the food moves down your throat ... After you have swallowed, when you are ready, take another bite. Take your time. Be curious about your experience ... notice how your body, mind, and heart feel now, in this moment.

Listening to Music While Staying Here

This is another exercise I developed with Louise Hayes (Black, 2016). I recommend that you ask the child's parent in advance if they consent to your playing music in the session with the child, as there may be cultural or religious restrictions on what type of music the child is permitted to listen to. For this exercise, play a song without giving any instructions in advance. If the child asks you what they should do, you might reply that they can notice their mind wondering what the rules are. After playing the song, ask the child what they were thinking about while listening to the song. Then invite the child to listen to the song again, and this time, to try to listen to it while staying here. After playing the song a second time, ask the child what they might have heard the second time that they did not hear the first time.

Moving Like Seaweed

I adapted this exercise from Amy Saltzman and Philippe Goldin (Saltzman & Goldin, 2008), and I generally use it with children up to the age of eight years (but use your judgment to determine whether it may be suitable for a child over the age of eight). For this exercise, give the child the option of lying down on the floor or carpet or remaining seated in their chair. Most of the children I have suggested this exercise to have been willing to try it and have chosen to lie down. (I have carpet in my office at school and in my private practice; if your office doesn't have carpet and you have a yoga mat, you might like to offer that the child lie on the mat instead of the floor.) I've found that when parents are in the therapy room with their child, they enjoy participating alongside their child (either lying on the floor or carpet or seated), and afterward, they have indicated that they are keen to practice the exercise at home together with their child, to remind the child how to use it. This exercise is a great way to teach children about the *stay here* process because the child learns about paying attention to movement while also noticing how they feel in their body, as well as noticing their thoughts and feelings. This exercise combines the *let it be* process with the *stay here* process, through just noticing. You will find a suggested script below, but feel free to change or adapt it:

Imagine that you are seaweed, lying on the sand at the bottom of the sea, with your back or feet holding you firmly in the sand. The waves are big and move quickly, making the seaweed sway from side to side. Imagine that your arms and legs are moving, as the water pushes you back and forth. You might choose to move your arms and legs, and sway your arms from side to side, or up and down. The waves become smaller and smaller, and the sea becomes really still and calm, with hardly any movement. Try to lie still now, as you imagine what resting like seaweed on the sand, under the sea, that doesn't move at all, would be like. While you are doing this, notice how you feel in your body, what you are thinking, and what you are feeling.

After doing this exercise, invite the child to think about situations where they might experience emotions such as stress, worry, or anger, and ask them whether they think that doing this exercise might help them to manage being upset or distressed. Some parents have informed me that after participating in this exercise alongside their child in the session, they encouraged the child to do the exercise at home when the child was distressed (for example, following arguments with siblings), and it was very effective for helping the child to calm down quickly, preventing further escalation of emotions.

Mindful Breathing

As a reminder, we read in chapter 3 that for experiential exercises, you can give the child the option of either closing their eyes or choosing a spot on the floor to focus on, to reduce the likelihood of distraction. I have found that this is a particularly good exercise to teach children who may be anxious and prone to experiencing panic attacks, as it often helps regulate their breathing, preventing them from hyperventilating. This exercise often empowers children by giving them tools they can use to help themselves quickly and discreetly, in order to cope with situations where they feel anxious, thereby reducing the likelihood of having a panic attack. I learned this exercise in a two-day workshop with Mike Twohig (Twohig, 2014) and adapted the script. You can use the script as follows, or you can adapt it:

Put your hands on your tummy, placing them flat, at either side of your belly. Take a couple of slow breaths, breathing in through your nose, feeling the cool air inside your nostrils, and slowly breathing out through your mouth. Then take another slow breath, in through your nose, and out through your mouth, and feel your tummy gently going in, then going out, like when a balloon is being blown up. If you are in a situation where you notice yourself becoming worried, this is something that you can do on your own to stay here, and help yourself calm down. You can do it all by yourself, and no one will know the reasons why you are doing it. You can do this at home, in the car, in class at school, or anywhere else when you feel that it might be helpful.

HELPFUL HINT

If the child you are using this exercise with experiences stress or anxiety, or has a specific phobia (such as dogs, bugs, or spiders), include the specific situation in which the child becomes stressed or anxious in the script, which may help make the exercise very relevant for them.

In addition to doing any of these experiential exercises in sessions, you can invite the child to complete the following worksheet in the session or take it home to complete. This worksheet can be downloaded in color from http://www.ne wharbinger.com/49760.

Worksheet 5: Staying Here

What are some activities you could try to do to practice staying here and really noticing what's going on around you, instead of being caught up in your thoughts (for example, listening to music, drawing, or painting)?

_____

_____

_____

What could you do to help yourself stay here and notice what's happening around you?

_____

_____

_____

_____

_____

Write down the days and times below when you could practice staying here, and include some activities you can do to practice this.

_____

_____

_____

_____

As we've discussed, it's extremely beneficial for the child to continue practicing the exercises between sessions. Let's consider how to give recommendations to children and their parents for doing *stay here* exercises at home, in order to practice and further develop this process.

Stay Here Exercises for Home

Toward the end of a session focused on the *stay here* process, I make sure to talk to the child about exercises they could do at home to practice staying here. If the child's parent has been sitting in the waiting room during the session, I ask the child to invite their parent (where appropriate) to join us in the therapy room so I can spend a few minutes informing the parent about the *stay here* process. Then I teach the parent how to use the *stay here* exercise at home that the child and I have done in the session, and I also give the parent suggestions of how they can encourage their child to practice staying here.

HELPFUL HINT

When recommending home tasks, try to choose some that you think the child might like to do. If you know the child loves art, then you might suggest painting or drawing while staying here, but if the child doesn't like art, suggest some alternative exercises instead. I like to suggest some home tasks that I know that the child will already be doing as part of their everyday routine, rather than only

---

suggesting *extra* tasks, which they might be reluctant to do.

For each exercise below, I've included some instructions so that you can see how I describe the exercises to the child and their parent, but you can make up your own scripts for these exercises, or modify the scripts I've provided. Let's look now at some everyday exercises that you can recommend to children and their parents. The child can do these at home on their own, or their parent might wish to do some of them together with the child.

Listening to Music

I recommend suggesting this to all children, including those with whom you have done the Listening to Music While Staying Here exercise in the session. You can introduce this exercise to the child as follows:

> *Try listening to some of your favorite music, really paying attention to the words, sounds, and different instruments. Try seeing whether you can hear anything in the music that you might not have heard before. If your attention drifts away, and you find yourself thinking about other things unrelated to the song, try gently bringing your attention back to listening to the music.*

Brushing Your Teeth

While we don't do toothbrushing as an actual exercise in sessions, I still suggest instructions for this to the child as well as their parent so that if they choose to try it at home, they know how to stay here while brushing their teeth. The following is an example of a script that I use when suggesting this exercise to children:

> *When you brush your teeth, try to notice the smell and taste of the toothpaste, the sensation and sound of the brush against your teeth, and the temperature of the water. Notice how the toothbrush feels in your hand, and whether you are holding it tightly, or loosely. You might see yourself in the mirror: try to watch your reflection, and notice that you are watching yourself, brushing your teeth. You might also notice the sink, faucet, and drain, being aware of the colors, texture, and anything else that might be on the sink, like soap. If your mind wanders to thoughts about what you will be doing today or tomorrow, or what you did today, try to bring your attention back to really noticing brushing your teeth.*

You might have observed that I used the phrase "notice that you are watching yourself," which introduces the child to the *notice yourself* process, and how they can combine *stay here* and *notice yourself.*

Painting or Drawing

You can suggest to the child that they try to practice staying here while doing a painting or drawing at home or at school. The child and their parent might enjoy sitting together at a table at home and each doing a painting or drawing, and you could suggest that afterward, they may wish to share their experiences with each other of trying to stay here while painting or drawing. You could use the following script, or make up your own:

If you do a painting, try to notice the sensation of your hand holding the brush, and the brush mixing the colors. As your brush touches the paper, try to notice how that feels too. Listen to the sounds as you wash the brush in water, and of the water lapping at the side of the cup/glass/jar. You might also like to paint using your fingers instead of a brush—you can notice the cool paint against your fingers and palm of your hand, feeling the sensation of your hand and fingers against the paper. If you use pencils instead of paint, notice the sensation of the pencil in your hand and against the paper, and also pay attention to the different colors you are drawing.

Eating Dinner with Your Family

This is the exercise that I like to recommend to children and parents more often than any other *stay here* exercise. I find that parents usually respond quite enthusiastically to this exercise (especially if they are the main cook at home, as doing this exercise might lead to greater appreciation for their cooking!). In my experience, lots of parents really like the idea of introducing quality, quiet time during dinner, without the noise of TV, screens, and phones, so engaging in this exercise may help bring this to fruition. I encourage parents to invite the child to teach it to the whole family once they are seated for dinner, in order to introduce to everyone in the family the skill of staying here while eating. I suggest to parents that they first give the child a chance to provide the instructions, and then provide help if needed. (You can download the sample script below from http://www.newharbinger.com/49760 and give the parent a copy to take home.) The parent might also need to ask other family members to listen while the child is speaking. I introduce this exercise as follows:

> *Invite everyone in the house to come to the table/counter and eat the meal together. Before starting to eat, tell everyone that you*

would like them to try a different way of eating from how everyone usually eats at your home. Ask your family to eat slowly, in silence, trying to notice the smells of the food, the colors, the textures, and the flavors. You can tell your family that when their minds drift away, they can try to notice this, and gently bring their attention back to the food. When everyone is finished eating, each person can have a turn to talk about their experience: What smells, colors, textures, and flavors did they notice? If the meal was something that they had eaten previously, did it taste the same, or did they notice anything different? If anyone wants to interrupt while someone else is talking, they can just notice that they wish to speak, and wait their turn. I recommend changing the order of people speaking each night so that each person gets a turn to speak first.

Staying Here for Falling Asleep

Often children will tell you that they have difficulty falling asleep because they can't get their brain or mind to stop working or they can't stop thinking or worrying. You can use the following script to help children who have difficulties falling asleep, or feel free to vary it:

When you get into bed, close your eyes, and listen to the sounds outside the room. Then *listen to the sounds inside the room, and listen to the sound of your breathing. If you notice your mind racing with thoughts, such as about what happened during the day, or what might happen tomorrow, try to gently bring your attention back to the sound of your breathing.*

This exercise can slow down children's thoughts in order to quiet and calm their mind so they can fall asleep. I have found that children respond really well to this exercise (and often yawn after I go over the instructions, indicating that they are quite relaxed by it). I recommend that you also try it yourself; if you find it helpful and wish to use it with the children you work with, you will be able to share your experiences with them.

Other activities that I recommend to children and their parents for practicing *stay here* at home (and that can also be used at school) are:

- listening to others
- reading
- playing a board/card game
- playing ball

For each of these exercises, I encourage the child to concentrate on the activity, and if they notice their mind drift away, they can gently bring their mind back to the activity.

Now let's turn to teaching the process of *notice yourself* to children.

Introducing Notice Yourself

When I introduce the *notice yourself* process to children, I define it as standing back and noticing yourself. I explain that it's a bit like when we look at ourselves in a mirror, where sometimes we see what we expected in our reflection, and other times we might be surprised by what we see. I add that when we notice ourselves, we might not actually have a *real* mirror. Instead, we can be in the middle of doing something, then we can stop and notice ourselves doing the action, without looking in an actual mirror. I find it helpful to provide children with an example like the following:

Imagine that you are sitting on the couch at home, and you have homework due the next day. You feel tired, and really don't want to get up from the couch to go to your room and do your homework. Your mind tells you to wait a few more minutes, then you'll get up. You notice that you are sitting on the couch, having the thought that you are tired, and not wanting to move to do homework: that's noticing yourself! You might choose to get up anyway, and go to your room, sit down at your desk, open your book, and start to do your work, because you don't want to fall behind in your schoolwork, and you know you have even more homework tomorrow night.

You might have noticed that I also included some of the other processes of the ACT Kidflex ("having the thought that" is the *let it go* process, "you might choose to get up anyway ... and start to do your work" is the *do what matters* process, and "because you don't want to fall behind in your schoolwork" is the *choose what matters* process). I include these to link *notice yourself* to some of the earlier processes I have taught the child, and show the child that noticing themself can help them to let it go, choose what matters, and do what matters, even when their mind tells them not to get up off the couch.

After introducing *notice yourself* to children, you might like to invite the child to participate in a *notice yourself* art exercise during the session. Below I provide some suggested exercises, but the possibilities are endless. For each one, I suggest that you provide the child with paper and a selection of markers, pencils, and oil pastels, which the child can choose from.

Notice Yourself Art Exercises

I recommend that you only do one art exercise in the session where you address *notice yourself*, so as not to be rushing the child to complete the exercises. For all art exercises, I highly recommend that you allow the child to choose which exercise to do, and do the same art exercise yourself alongside the child (which may reduce the chance of the child's becoming distracted if you're doing a different exercise, or feeling that they chose the wrong exercise).

HELPFUL HINT

It's important that you allow enough time for an art exercise (I usually find that about thirty minutes works well). If you don't have much time left at the end of a session, don't start an art exercise and rush through it, as it's less likely to be meaningful for the child. Instead, leave it for the start of the next session.

After the child has finished their artwork, invite them to tell you about what they've created, letting them know that they don't have to discuss their work if they don't wish to. Then you can share your artwork with the child, ensuring that what you disclose to the child is appropriate (see therapist self-disclosure in chapter 1).

You may wish to invite the child to choose one of the following art exercises to complete in the session.

Under the Sea

This exercise is adapted from a Baba Ram Dass metaphor. You can introduce it to the child using the following script (available for downloading at http://www.newharbinger.com/49 760), or you can adapt it:

The sea contains different sized waves: sometimes it's calm and still, at other times it's stormy. The sea contains waves, sand, fish, seaweed, and shells, and sometimes other things too, like dolphins and whales. These are all part of the sea, but they are not the sea. Sometimes it can be really hard to see the sea through all the waves, but the sea is still always there. In the same way, we have lots of different thoughts and feelings, but we are not our thoughts and feelings. We don't feel the same way all the time, and sometimes it's really hard to notice ourselves having these thoughts and feelings, because of how strong they feel. For this exercise, you can draw a picture of under the sea, and you might like to include waves that you could write your thoughts and feelings on. You might also like to draw a treasure chest under the sea that contains all the things that matter to you, or anything else you'd like to include.

You may have noticed that writing thoughts and feelings on waves is a *let it go* exercise, and the treasure chest represents the *choose what matters* process, which I included in order to teach the child how to combine *let it go, choose what matters,* and *notice yourself.*

Flower with Petals

I developed this exercise when I was working with five-year-old Rosie during her first year of school. Rosie had generalized anxiety disorder, and she was anxious about leaving her parents at the school gate and walking into school and her classroom without them. She was also frightened of Benjamin, an older student at school, and she hid in the restroom at recess and lunch to avoid him, instead of playing on the playground with her friends. Rosie experienced diarrhea when she was anxious, and she called out for her parents while sleeping. When she had a conflict with friends at school, she avoided her friends.

For this exercise, I invited Rosie to draw a flower with lots of petals. Then I asked her if she could write down all the things she was afraid of and worried about, with one thought on each petal. Rosie struggled with spelling, so she asked me to write the words for her.

Rosie dictated the following thoughts:

- "I am scared of Benjamin at school."
- "I have to hide in the restroom."
- "I want to go to the playground but I can't because Benjamin might be there."
- "When I go to the cafeteria at school, I have to look for Benjamin, and hide if he's there."
- "I miss having fun at school."
- "I want to be happy."

- "I want to walk into school by myself."
- "I want to play hide and seek with my friends but I can't because Benjamin might be there."

I wrote Rosie's thoughts on the petals—one thought per petal, but as there were so many thoughts, I needed to ask Rosie to draw more petals—then I asked her to describe each part of the flower, telling me what she could see. After this, I asked Rosie, "Is the flower only the petals, or does the flower have more parts than just the petals?" Rosie replied that there were more parts, and I asked her to describe what else she could see. She told me about the middle of the flower, the stem, and the sharp thorns. I told Rosie that her thoughts and feelings are like the petals, and that she is like the middle of the flower and the stem. The petals are one part of the flower, but they are not the whole flower: even when the petals change, the stem stays the same, including when it grows and becomes taller. I told Rosie that, like the flower, she stays the same, even when she grows.

Sunglasses with Labels

I created this exercise when working with Martin, a six-year-old autistic boy who had several different fears. Before starting this exercise, I recommend that you first show the child an actual pair of sunglasses (or a photo) to explain what lenses are in case they don't know the word. After showing Martin my own sunglasses, I invited him to draw a pair of sunglasses, then think about all of the things he was afraid of, and write these thoughts and feelings as labels on the lenses of the glasses. You may need to offer to write for the child if they have writing or spelling difficulties and may not feel comfortable writing.

Martin wrote the following labels on the glasses:

- "I am scared of dogs."
- "I worry when I have a new teacher."
- "I am scared at night in my bedroom."
- "I am frightened in the auditorium because of the big screen."
- "I am scared when it's too noisy at school."

After Martin finished drawing and writing, I had a discussion with him about his drawing, which is detailed in the following transcript:

Therapist: What would happen if we wore these sunglasses and always looked at the labels stuck on the lenses—would we be able to see anything else other than the labels?

Martin: No, we'd just be looking at the labels, but we wouldn't be able to read them, as they'd be back to front.

Therapist: That's a really good point! What would happen if we tried to walk around wearing these glasses, and we always looked at the labels?

Martin: It would be hard to see, and we'd probably bump into things and fall over.

Therapist: What would happen if we just noticed the labels, but didn't try to take them off, and looked past them, looking through the lenses, and watched all the things that we could see, some close and some far away?

Martin: We'd probably be able to see better and have less falls, and we wouldn't step on other peoples' feet.

Therapist: I think you're correct! Would we notice anything that we haven't seen before?

Martin: Yes, and there might also be things that aren't there all the time, which is why we might not have seen them before.

Therapist: Wow, that's another really good point! We could try just noticing the labels, and noticing what else we can see. Then, we can also try noticing that we are noticing the lenses, the labels, and everything that we can see through the lenses.

Martin: Okay, I could try that.

In addition to using art exercises for the *notice yourself* process, you'll want to use experiential exercises in sessions to further strengthen the child's understanding of the *notice yourself* process. We'll cover these next.

Notice Yourself Experiential Exercises

Give the child the option of either closing their eyes or choosing a spot on the floor to focus on, so that they are not looking around the room during these exercises and unable to concentrate. I recommend that you give the child this option for all of the following experiential exercises.

Still Quiet Ship

I learned this exercise in a two-day workshop given by Lisa Coyne (Coyne, 2011), and I have found that it helps children to develop *notice yourself* skills by visualizing their thoughts and seeing them as separate from themselves. It also uses the *let it go* process by teaching children to place their thoughts on a storm cloud. I have modified the script slightly, which you can use as follows or adapt. Afterward, you can invite the child to talk about their experience, if they wish to.

Close your eyes, and imagine you are in a huge sailing ship that is heavy and safe in the water. Outside the ship's windows it's stormy, and the sky is filled with dark clouds. Imagine that your thoughts are the storm clouds, which you can watch safely from inside your ship. Each time a thought shows up in your mind, place it on a storm cloud, watching it move in the wind. Watch the storm clouds, noticing what they look like—whether they are moving quickly or slowly, and whether there's lightening, thunder, or rain. Try to notice yourself, inside a ship, watching the storm clouds.

The Beach

I developed this exercise based on the Still Quiet Ship (adapted from Coyne, 2011) exercise above, and it is also similar to the Waves on the Ocean (adapted from Hayes & Smith, 2005) exercise we read about in chapter 3 for the *let it go* process. This exercise not only introduces the child to *notice yourself*, but it also helps them learn how to combine *notice yourself* with *let it go* (through placing thoughts onto the waves). If you have already used the Waves on the Ocean exercise, you could still use this exercise with the same child if you wish (but in a different session from the one in which you introduced the *let it go* process).

The following is an example of how you can use The Beach exercise (but, as always, feel free to adapt this script):

Imagine that you are standing on a beach, right by the water. The waves roll onto the shore, some strong and others gentle. As you notice the waves, try to also notice whatever thoughts are showing up in your mind, and imagine that they are like waves that come to the shore—some are strong and others are gentle. Your mind comes up with lots of different thoughts, just like the ocean has lots of different waves. Some days the ocean is really still and calm, and on other days it's really stormy with rough, big waves that crash on the shore. Sometimes there's a mixture of small and large waves. As you're imagining yourself standing by the water, imagine that you can place whatever thoughts that your mind comes up with onto the waves, and watch those waves roll out to sea. If your mind comes up with another thought, gently place that one on a wave too. Try to notice yourself standing by the water, gently placing whatever your mind comes up with onto the waves.

Watching a Movie of Your Life

This is my favorite *notice yourself* exercise, which I adapted from Coyne and Murrell's (2009) Forgiving a Friend, Forgiving Yourself exercise and Sawyer (personal correspondence, Sawyer, 2012). The exercise entails having the child imagine that they are at a movie theater, watching a movie about their life. I've used Watching a Movie of Your Life with children from the age of seven years and older. If you want to try using it with five- and six-year-olds, I would suggest making it briefer, so the child doesn't lose concentration. You could also focus the movie on a very specific situation the child is having difficulties with (for example, difficulties making friends at school, being teased, being unsure of whom to play with when their friends are away from school, and worries about schoolwork).

If you don't have a lot of time left in the session, I don't recommend doing this exercise, because it works best when you are not rushed. Instead, leave it for the start of the next session so you can give the child plenty of time to adjust to being in the therapy room after the exercise (which is especially helpful if they close their eyes during the exercise), and also to ensure that there is sufficient time for the child to share their experience with you, if they wish to.

HELPFUL HINT

One of the reasons I love the Watching a Movie of Your Life exercise is that you can be really creative with it. Take your time with the first part of the exercise (before the movie begins), and don't be tempted to rush: give the child time to *really* imagine that they are at the movie theater, which will help make their experience more powerful and the exercise more effective

---

Let's look at a case example that shows how I used this exercise with a child.

Case Example: Lola, Eight Years Old

Lola was feeling depressed and had thoughts of wanting to end her life. She shared these thoughts and feelings with her parents, who immediately took her to her family doctor, who referred Lola to me. Lola also experienced anxiety and worried a lot, especially if she arrived late anywhere. She had very high expectations of herself academically and also as a dancer, and put a lot of pressure on herself not to make mistakes, which lowered her mood even more. She was very critical of herself. Her coping strategy when she felt sad or worried was to isolate herself from her family for a lengthy period of time, which tended to make her feel worse. She and her mother had a conflictual relationship, and when they argued, Lola felt sad for several days.

The following transcript shows how I introduced the Watching a Movie of Your Life exercise with Lola:

Therapist: Lola, I'd like to try an exercise with you, which involves you imagining that you're at the movies, and are watching a movie about your life. If you think you'd like to try it, I'll briefly tell you what it involves, and then you can decide whether you'd like to participate. If you *don't* wish to participate, that's absolutely okay, and I'll let you know some other exercises that you can choose from.

Lola: I'm okay to hear about it.

Therapist: The exercise involves us sitting here, and I'll talk to you and ask you to imagine that you're watching a movie about your life. You will watch yourself doing things in the movie, and afterward, if you are comfortable with this, I'll ask you some questions about what you saw in the movie.

Lola: It sounds unusual, but sure, I'm happy to try it.

Therapist: Great, thank you. For this exercise, you can close your eyes, or if you'd rather leave them open, please choose a spot on the floor to focus on, so that you can concentrate on what I'm saying and aren't looking around the room and feeling distracted.

Lola: (closes her eyes)

Therapist: I'm wondering if you and your family ever go to the movie theater to watch a movie, and if you do, which movie theater do you go to?

Lola: We go to Movie City.

Therapist: And when you go to the movies, do your parents bring some snacks and drinks from home, or do they buy something at the movie theater?

Lola: We usually make popcorn at home, and probably take chips or chocolate, and my parents buy us a drink there.

Therapist: Now I want you to imagine that you're sitting back in the comfy seats at Movie City, eating popcorn, and maybe some chips or chocolate, and having a drink. Do you remember what color the seats are at Movie City?

Lola: The seats are red and really soft, like velvet.

Therapist: Imagine that you're sitting back in your seat at the movie theater, feeling really comfortable, and you're going to be watching a movie about your life. This movie doesn't have a title, so you get to come up with the title.

Lola: Ooh that's going to be hard! How do I know what to call it?

Therapist: I promise that there's no wrong or right title—you can call it whatever feels right for you.

Lola: But I *really* don't know what to call it!

Therapist: Would something like "Lola's Life" or "About Lola" seem right for you?

Lola: I want to call it "The Story of Lola."

Therapist: That sounds like a great title; good job!

Lola: Thanks *(smiles)*.

HELPFUL HINT

In the next part of this exercise, continue speaking directly to the child, inviting them to imagine watching the movie of themself, but finish taking them through watching the movie before asking them any questions so they can remain focused on watching the pretend movie.

Watch out for the places where I encourage her to "watch Lola" in the movie, instead of saying "Watch yourself." I do this to remind Lola to watch herself, and also to build some separation between Lola who is watching the movie and Lola who is *in* the movie. This will hopefully help Lola develop the skill to notice herself, which she will be able to use outside of therapy sessions.

Therapist: I'd like you to try to imagine that you're sitting in your seat at the movie theater, watching the movie "The Story of Lola." Perhaps your parents, brother, and sister are with you. The movie begins, but it doesn't have to begin when you were born—it can begin wherever you'd like it to.

I'd like you to watch Lola in the movie; perhaps you're watching her at school, at home, and at dance school. As you watch Lola in the movie, I want you to try to notice yourself sitting in your chair, how you feel in your body, and what you're thinking and feeling. Watch what Lola in the movie does, and who she talks to, and see if you can work out from the look on her face how she's feeling.

I'd like you to also pay attention to whether you think what Lola does in the movie is helpful for her, or whether you think she should try doing some things differently. You might see Lola going to dance lessons and performing in concerts—watch her, and notice if your mind makes any judgments about her.

You might also notice what happens when Lola's mom picks her up from dance lessons—try to listen to their conversation, particularly how Lola reacts. You might notice what happens when Lola arrives home, and how she interacts with her family. You might see Lola's new puppy, Cookie—watch whether there's any difference in how Lola greets Cookie compared to how she greets the rest of her family. Watch what Lola does at home, who she talks to or doesn't talk to, and what she does in her room. Notice yourself sitting in the seat at Movie City, watching the movie.

Now I want you to imagine that the movie pauses—it doesn't end, so you can still see what's on the screen, but it's stopped playing any more scenes. Try to imagine that you get up from your seat by yourself, and walk past everyone to the front of the movie theater, toward the screen. Imagine that you step inside the screen, and slowly walk up to Lola in the movie. Notice how you're feeling inside your body, and what you're thinking and feeling. Imagine that you could go up to Lola in the movie and give her some advice! Tell her what you think she should do when she feels sad and starts to think about ending her life, and whether you think she should do anything differently.

HELPFUL HINT

At this point in the exercise, pause to give the child time to sit with their thoughts and feelings (let it be).

Therapist: (continuing) When you're ready, try to imagine that you say goodbye to Lola in the movie (I paused again, allowing Lola time to comprehend this idea to let her thoughts and feelings be—this uses the let it be process). Notice how you feel in your body, and notice yourself noticing all of this. Imagine that you walk away from Lola in the movie, head back toward the screen, then walk through the screen and back to your seat, and sit down next to your family (I paused again, really giving Lola time and space *to process this).* Then, the movie ends and the curtains close. The lights come on and people start leaving the movie theater.

When you're ready, open your eyes, and come back to being here in the room (or online) with me.

HELPFUL HINT

At this point in the exercise, I recommend that you stay silent for a few minutes, really giving the child time to adjust to being back in the room, to adjust to the lighting if they had closed their eyes, and to sit with and process what's occurred for them. In this way, you are modeling the *let it be* process.

Once you've given the child a few minutes, you might wish to ask them if you may ask some questions about their experience.

Therapist: Lola, would it be okay if I ask you some questions about the exercise?

Lola: Sure!

Therapist: Thank you. How was that exercise for you?

Lola: At the start it was hard to imagine looking at myself, but then I could do it.

Therapist: Was there anything you saw that surprised you?

Lola: Definitely! I, I mean Lola, puts so much pressure on herself. Instead of just enjoying dance classes and having fun with her friends, she looked so serious, and angry when she made mistakes. Who cares if you make mistakes at dance class, right? And she looked miserable right before the dance concert. I've been practicing so hard for months for the concert, but I just want to enjoy myself. But Lola looked so scared that she might make a mistake! She thinks that her teacher will be angry or disappointed if she messes up. But I know that's not true; her teacher is really kind.

Therapist: And what did you notice when Lola's mom picked her up from dance lessons?

Lola: Lola was so mean to her mom! My mom, I mean Lola's mom, was so nice, and asked her how school and dance class were, but Lola just ignored her and looked out the window.

Therapist: Do you think that ignoring her mom was helpful for her?

Lola: No, I think it made me, I mean Lola, feel even worse, and sadder.

Therapist: Did you notice anything about when Lola arrived home?

Lola: She was so happy to see Cookie, but she ignored her family. When Lola's dad got angry at Lola for not picking up Cookie's poop in the yard, Lola cried and went to her room for hours, missing dinner.

Therapist: What did you notice when Lola was in her room?

Lola: She started thinking that she'd be better off if she was no longer alive, but she also thought about how sad her family would be, *especially* her mom.

At this point, I pause for a few moments, allowing Lola time to sit with what she had observed (this also encourages Lola to use the *let it be* process). If I change the topic at this point, I might mistakenly give Lola the impression that I feel uncomfortable hearing her thoughts of ending her life, and I might also incorrectly convey the idea that the topic should be changed or avoided, in response to my *own* discomfort. This would not teach Lola to be flexible (remember that the aim of the ACT Kidflex is *I am flexible*). Instead, I take care to just sit with what Lola is telling me (also demonstrating my own use of the *let it be* process), and I maintain eye contact to show that I'm really listening to her (demonstrating that I'm using the *stay here* process).

Therapist: Were you able to imagine that you could step into the screen and speak to Lola, and give her any advice?

Lola: Yes.

Therapist: How did it feel in your body, and how's it feeling now thinking about it?

Lola: My tummy felt funny, likes waves, like when I get nervous—it's actually doing that a little now. I told Lola to stop taking everything so seriously, be nicer to her mom, and tell her how she really feels instead of keeping everything to herself. I also told her to spend more time cuddling Cookie, because that always makes me feel better! Also, I told Lola that if she wants to go to her room when she's sad, she should let her mom know how she's feeling instead, especially when she starts thinking about what it would be like if she was no longer alive. Her mom might be able to help her.

Therapist: You're doing really well. What was it like when you said goodbye to Lola in the movie?

Lola: I felt sad, like I didn't want to leave her there, but I know that she'll be okay because her family really cares about her a lot. And she has Cookie too.

Therapist: Lola, you did a great job with that exercise. I've actually done it myself (*disclosing my own use of the exercise may increase the likelihood of Lola using it outside of sessions*), and I know it can be really hard to imagine watching yourself. You can do the movie exercise on your own any time you feel sad, or upset, or angry, or when you're not sure if the way you're dealing with your thoughts and feelings is helping you. You can close your eyes for a couple of minutes and watch yourself, and notice whether what you're doing is helpful, or whether there's some advice that you might be able to give yourself.

Lola: Okay, thank you so much.

Therapist: You're very welcome.

Let's look at a worksheet now that you can invite the child to complete after finishing this exercise, or, if they seem fatigued after the exercise, you could ask if they would like to take it home to complete. (I recommend that you only give this worksheet to the child if you actually did the exercise with them in a session; otherwise, they are unlikely to know what to write.) The worksheet is available for download in color from http://www.newharbinger.com/497 60.

Worksheet 6: Watching a Movie of Your Life

Imagine that you go to the movie theater and watch a movie of your life. You get to write the title and watch yourself when you have difficulties coping with your thoughts and feelings (perhaps at home, school, or other places).

Think about some things you might have noticed the person playing you in the movie doing that aren't helpful, or perhaps think about some things the person should try doing differently.

If you could tell the person playing you in the movie something that might help them cope with their thoughts and feelings, what would you say to them?

Now draw a movie screen below, and on the screen write some things the person playing you could do differently, so they can cope with their thoughts and feelings better.

Next we'll look at feedback I gave Lola's mom and recommendations for home.

Working with Lola's Parent

Apart from the first session, where Lola asked her mom to join us, Lola didn't want her mom to attend her sessions, so her mom sat in the waiting room on each occasion. About ten minutes before the end of each session, I asked Lola what information she was comfortable having me share with her mom. Then I outlined to Lola how I planned to give her mom feedback about the strategies that I'd addressed with Lola during the session, as well as how I felt Lola was progressing. On each occasion, Lola and I were able to reach an agreement about what information I would share with her mom. (Note that whenever I gave feedback to Lola's mom, I always did so in front of Lola so she didn't worry about what was said about her.)

Although in our first session, Lola's mother had informed me that Lola had experienced thoughts of wanting to end her life, Lola had denied having thoughts of any plans or intent to end her life. Lola also reported that the thoughts of wanting to end her life ceased after our first session. As such, there were no occasions when I needed to breach Lola's confidentiality and inform her mother of anything against Lola's will.

Lola and her mom had a fairly conflictual relationship, and Lola was very guarded with what she shared with her, as she felt that her mom always tried to fix her problems—by offering solutions and telling her what she should do differently. This infuriated Lola, who felt her mom was criticizing her. She just wanted her mom to listen to her and reassure her that things would be okay. In the two sessions on *stay here* and *notice yourself,* we role-played Lola telling her mom what support she wanted from her, and I encouraged Lola to try to stay here: by paying particular attention to her posture, how she was feeling in her body, and what her mind was thinking ("what your mind is thinking" is also a reminder of the *let it go* process). I also encouraged Lola to notice herself participating in the role-play and notice herself noticing what she was feeling and thinking.

At the end of both sessions, I invited Lola to ask her mom to join us. I explained the *stay here* and *notice yourself* processes and how she could encourage Lola to stay here and notice herself when Lola is upset, as well as when things are going well. Lola told her mom that when she shared how she was feeling, she wanted her mom to support her by telling her that everything would be okay instead of telling her how to make things better. Lola's mom became teary hearing this and told Lola how proud she was that Lola had expressed to her how she really felt. She also told Lola that she was willing to change, and just listen, without trying to fix things (this is a beautiful example of Lola's mom using the *let it be* process herself!). I suggested to Lola's mom that she could also practice staying here and noticing herself when Lola approached her for support, and she could also teach Lola's dad to do this, which she agreed to do.

Lola responded very well to therapy. I saw her on eight occasions, and on each occasion, I asked her to rate her mood on a scale from 1–10. Her self-ratings of her mood improved significantly, and her mom agreed with Lola's ratings. In sessions, Lola became more carefree and looked visibly relaxed and happier. She also reported significant decreases in self-criticism and worrying.

Suggestions for Parents

When giving parents suggestions for how they can help their child to practice *stay here* and *notice yourself,* I make sure to recommend strategies that parents can use as part of everyday activities. For example, you can recommend to parents that they encourage their family to practice staying here while eating dinner, and you might like to offer the parent a copy of the Eating Dinner with Your Family script provided earlier in this chapter (and available as a free tool online) for that exercise.

Parents can also practice staying here while going for a walk with their child—the parent and child can point out pretty or unusual flowers to each other, pausing to look at them or smell them if appropriate. They can also stop to watch a butterfly, or look at an interesting bush, or leaves on a tree, noticing changes in color or size. If it's fall and there are leaves on the ground, parents can encourage their child to listen to the crunching sound as they walk on them. Both parents and child might enjoy watching the sunset together, and the parent can suggest that the child look at the different shapes of the clouds, colors in the sky, and changing light as the sun sets. This is one of my favorite *stay here* exercises, and it has become a regular and greatly enjoyed ritual that I do with my own children.

Parents might also like to practice staying here when they are cooking, and they can encourage their child to notice the change in colors, textures, and smells of the food while it's being cooked. When parents are helping their child to practice staying here, they can try to notice themselves as well as their child staying here, and also encourage their child to notice themself. Parents can also suggest that their child try to set some time aside each day where they slow down, notice what's around them, and try to notice themself noticing, and they can offer to help their child select a suitable time for this.

Conclusion

In this chapter, we've covered the processes of *stay here* and *notice yourself*. You have introduced the child to these processes in order to help them learn to be present and aware of what they are experiencing and to stand back and watch themself. This includes observing themself in situations where they experience difficulties and noticing whether what they do is helpful or not. You have also introduced them to exercises and provided recommendations for simple exercises they can do on their own in order to practice these processes and incorporate them into their everyday, regular routine.

The *stay here* and *notice yourself* exercises build on the other processes we have already read about in chapters 3 and 4 (*let it be, let it go, choose what matters,* and *do what matters*), which complete all of the processes in the ACT Kidflex. The next chapter focuses on introducing self-compassion (which we'll refer to as *be kind and caring to yourself*) to children and how to use *be kind and caring to yourself* exercises in conjunction with the ACT Kidflex.

CHAPTER 6

Be Kind and Caring to Yourself

You've addressed all of the processes of the ACT Kidflex: *let it be, let it go, choose what matters, do what matters, stay here,* and *notice yourself.* In addition to learning about the ACT Kidflex, some children you work with might also benefit from learning about self-compassion, which is commonly referred to as "ACT's best friend." With children, we refer to self-compassion as "be kind and caring to yourself" to make it easier for them to understand. In this chapter, we'll look at how to introduce *be kind and caring to yourself* to children, use *be kind and caring to yourself* exercises in sessions, and recommend exercises to children and their parents for practice at home.

Linking Be Kind and Caring to Yourself to the ACT Kidflex

Not every child you work with will need to be introduced to *be kind and caring to yourself,* as they may already be kind and caring to themself when they experience problems or difficulties and be skilled in its use. If you notice that a child is critical of themself, blames themself, or has very high expectations of themself and puts a lot of pressure on themself, then introducing them to *be kind and caring to yourself* might be helpful. In some cases, you may need to ask the child whether they are critical of themself, give themself a hard time, or speak to themself in a mean way.

Early in my training, I wasn't sure whether I should wait until I finished addressing all of the ACT Kidflex processes before introducing *be kind and caring to yourself,* or whether I should introduce this while addressing the ACT Kidflex processes. I quickly realized that it's not confusing for the child to be introduced to *be kind and caring to yourself* alongside the ACT Kidflex, and your sessions won't appear clunky. You can introduce it in the same session where you address one or two ACT Kidflex process. However, if you wish to do an experiential exercise (such as one provided below) with the child to introduce *be kind and caring to yourself,* then I recommend that you devote an entire session to it; this way you won't overload the child with too much information and you'll have sufficient time to address *be kind and caring to yourself.* You likely won't use every exercise in this chapter with the same child, so choose the ones that you think will be most suitable for your client.

Often, a child will say something self-critical when I'm addressing a process (or two) of the ACT Kidflex (such as during a session where I'm introducing them to *let it be, let it go,* or *notice yourself*). If there isn't sufficient time remaining in that session to introduce *be kind and caring to yourself,* I make a note in their file to introduce it in the next session.

In other cases, I may determine that the need to address *be kind and caring to yourself* is immediate. For example, the child may be very self-critical and have impossibly high expectations of themself; or they may have difficulty regulating their emotions, and as a result they experience panic attacks, or school refusal, or engage in self-harming. I then stop addressing the ACT Kidflex and shift to a *be kind and caring to yourself* exercise (this also demonstrates my *own* flexibility, which is good to model to the child). If you are addressing a particular ACT Kidflex process and then want to shift to *be kind and caring to yourself,* I recommend saying something like "I was going to do an exercise about letting go of our thoughts now, but I'd like to introduce you to *be kind and caring to yourself* instead. We'll do the letting go of our thoughts exercise if we have enough time afterward; if not, we'll look at it next time." Otherwise, pivoting away from the ACT Kidflex for a session might be confusing for the child.

> ## HELPFUL HINT
>
> If you're not sure whether there's a need to introduce the child to *be kind and caring to yourself*, you can try to engage the child in a *be kind and caring to yourself* exercise and see how they respond. Ask the child if they are critical of themselves or if their mind sometimes says mean things to them. (The phrase "if your mind sometimes says" is a reminder of or introduction to the ACT Kidflex process *let it go*.)

You might discover that they aren't self-critical, and they are already being kind and caring to themselves. That's great! When this occurs, you can return to addressing the processes of the ACT Kidflex, or, if you have already sufficiently covered the ACT processes with them, you could ask if there's anything else they wish to talk about it or would like help with. If there isn't, it might be time to suggest to the child and their parent that you finish working with the child.

Introducing Be Kind and Caring to Yourself

When introducing *be kind and caring to yourself*, I ask children what they think being kind and caring to themselves means. Often, children talk about what being kind and caring to *others* means, rather than to themselves, which might indicate they're not very kind and caring to themselves. It can be helpful to give an example, such as "You might be doing something that you find very hard, such as schoolwork, practicing for a recital or play, learning to play an instrument, or training for a sport. Speaking to yourself in a very kind and caring way would involve saying very nice and kind things to yourself, without saying anything mean or nasty, or telling yourself off."

HELPFUL HINT

To help children learn how to be kind and caring to themselves, ask them what words and type of voice would sound caring. If they aren't sure, you could suggest that when they are having a problem or difficulty—and also when things are going well—they can tell themselves in a calm voice that they are trying very hard, doing the best they can, will be able to get themselves through this, and won't feel like this forever.

To further help the child understand the concept of being kind and caring to themself, I often ask something like the following:

"Can you think of someone in your life who speaks to you in a very kind and caring way, and really supports you when you find things really difficult? Perhaps this is a family member, or a friend, or a teacher? The person you think of could also be someone from your past."

The child might tell you about someone very kind and caring who is currently in their life, or someone who has passed away (such as a grandparent, parent, aunt, or uncle). If this occurs, you could ask the child if they can recall some of the things the person said to them that were kind and caring.

You can also add, "If you don't have anyone in your life like that, or you haven't had someone in your life in the past like that, take a few moments to think about what it would be like to have someone in your life like that. (Pause, allowing the child some time to think about this.) What would you imagine they might say to you when you are having problems or difficulties, or when you aren't being very kind to yourself?"

Another approach is to ask the child, "Can you imagine what your pet might say to you if it could talk? What would your pet say about how you have been treating yourself, and what might your pet say to you?" If the child is able to imagine what their pet might say to them, you could suggest that when they are experiencing problems or difficulties, or notice that they are being unkind to themselves, they could think about what their pet might say to them.

Be Kind and Caring to Yourself Exercises

We'll look now at some experiential exercises you can do with children in sessions to teach *be kind and caring to yourself*. Most of these exercises can be used with children aged five to twelve years (I'll let you know which ones I don't recommend for use with five- to six-year-olds). You can select one or two exercises that you think will be most suitable for helping the child learn *be kind and caring to yourself* or that you think they are most likely to engage with. If you're not sure, you can select a few and briefly explain each exercise to the child, then invite them to choose one or two they'd like to participate in.

The Two Coaches

I find that young children (around five to eight years) and older children (around nine to twelve years) respond well to this exercise, which I adapted from Paul Gilbert's "Two Teachers Vignette" (Gilbert, 2009). This is one of my favorite *be kind and caring to yourself* exercises. You can invite the child to participate in this exercise, letting them know that you will ask them to imagine themselves doing something where they receive coaching from two different coaches, and then, if they are willing, you will ask them some questions about their experience. If the child agrees to participate, you can begin by asking if they play a sport, or an instrument, or have performed in a play, musical, or dance. If they can't think of something, ask if they've ever done something where they were coached, and include that activity in the exercise to make it relevant for them. If the child hasn't been coached before, ask them to think of something a child might receive coaching for, then use that as the example. Having a concrete example of something they or another child might be coached in helps children visualize this exercise and understand it better, which may lead to greater engagement.

To do this exercise, ask the child to imagine what a very critical coach would say to them, and how they would feel and perform. Then ask the child to imagine what a very kind and caring coach might say to them, how that would feel and how they would perform. Afterward, ask the child about their experiences of the exercise, and whether they noticed any difference in their performance with the two coaches. Ask the child which kind of coach they are more similar to, and how they might start speaking to themself in a more kind and caring way.

To get a better sense of how to use this exercise, we'll look at a transcript of a session with a ten-year-old client of mine named

Mark—an avid tennis player—where I used The Two Coaches exercise. (Feel free to replace tennis with something else that's more relevant for the child, and to adapt this script further in any way you like.) Mark was the shortest child in his grade, and his two younger brothers were taller than him. He struggled with body image and had become very self-conscious about his height, as many people thought he was the youngest in his family. His parents wanted me to see him to try to help him improve his self-esteem.

Therapist: For this exercise, you can either close your eyes or keep them open. If you prefer to keep your eyes open, I recommend that you focus on a spot on the floor, in order to concentrate. Imagine now that you are playing tennis, and your coach is watching you. Sometimes you hit the ball out of the court; sometimes you miss hitting it, or you hit it into the net. This coach is really mean, and gets angry, telling you off whenever they think you aren't playing well. Notice how you feel when the coach tells you off, and notice the expression on your face, and what you do after they tell you off. Notice whether you look like you're enjoying playing tennis, and whether you think that you're playing well.

Now, imagine that you had a *different* kind of coach: one who had a very kind and gentle voice, and was always calm. This coach *always* told you they could see how hard you were trying, no matter how you played. They told you how you could improve, and you felt like they *really* cared about teaching you, and helping you become a better tennis player. Notice how you feel when this coach tells you how hard you're trying, and notice the expression on your face when this coach talks to you in a really kind and caring way, and encourages you, and notice what you do after. Notice whether you look like you're enjoying playing tennis, and whether you're playing better or worse with this coach.

Notice whatever thoughts and feelings your mind is having *(this reminds or introduces Mark to the ACT Kidflex notice yourself process—see chapter 5 for further detail)* about both these types of coaches, about playing tennis, about yourself, and about anything else that your mind comes up with *(the phrase "your mind comes up with" reminds or introduces Mark to the ACT Kidflex let it go process—see chapter 3 for further detail).* When you're ready, open your eyes and come back to being here in the room *(or online)* with me.

HELPFUL HINT

After this portion of the Two Coaches exercise, allow the child a few minutes to sit with their thoughts and feelings (this models the ACT Kidflex *let it be* process—see chapter 3 for further detail) and adjust to being in the room with you, and possibly to having their eyes open, before asking them questions.

Therapist: Mark, would it be okay if I ask you a few questions about that exercise?

Mark: Sure.

Therapist: What was it like trying to imagine having two different coaches?

Mark: I really didn't want to be playing tennis when the first coach was mean, but I liked being there with the second coach.

Therapist: Was there any difference in how you played when you had the two different coaches?

Mark: I actually did worse with the first coach. I thought that I'd play well with someone telling me off, but they were *really* mean. I was scared the coach would be angry if I missed the ball or hit it out of the court, or served it into the net, and I ended up playing really badly—much worse than I'm capable of. I'd probably stop playing tennis if I had to keep having this coach, because I wouldn't enjoy playing.

Therapist: How was your performance with the kind and caring coach?

Mark: I *definitely* played better, because they told me I was doing a good job, and they also gave me tips on how to improve, which was really helpful.

Therapist: You did really well Mark. Now I'd like to invite you to think about how you've been speaking to yourself, especially when things are difficult for you. Which type of coach do you think you are more similar to—the mean coach, or the kind and caring coach?

Mark: I wouldn't have said the mean coach earlier, but now I realize that I'm actually more similar to the mean coach, even though I don't want to be like them.

Therapist: Do you think that speaking to yourself in a mean way is working for you, and helping you? (*This is a reminder of the question in the ACT case conceptualization template in chapter 2, which may help Mark be willing to try speaking to himself in a kind and caring way.)*

Mark: No.

Therapist: Would you be willing to try speaking to yourself in a kind and caring way, and seeing if that was more helpful?

Mark: I'm happy to give it a try.

Therapist: What words could you use to speak to yourself?

Mark: I could let myself know that it's not my fault that things are hard for me, that I'm doing the best I can, and that any other person my age would also find this really tough.

Therapist: They're great things to say to yourself.

To make this even more effective, ask the child *when* it might be helpful to try to talk to themselves in a kind and caring way, and whether there's anything that might make this difficult. If the child does foresee any possible difficulties, ask what they could do that might help. If they aren't sure, you can offer some suggestions, such as saying something kind and caring to themself each afternoon or evening when they come home from school, or each night before they go to sleep.

After doing The Two Coaches exercise, you could offer the child some pencils or a pen and invite them to complete the following worksheet about the kind and caring coach. The worksheet reinforces the exercise, and I find that it can be helpful for children to complete it during the session so they have a visual reminder of what they've learned in the session. If they don't wish to do a drawing on the worksheet, ask if they'd prefer to just write out some kind and caring statements on it. The child can complete the worksheet in the session or take it home to complete under the supervision of a parent. If the child agrees, ask them afterward if they would like to take the worksheet home, and perhaps put it on the wall in their bedroom, to remind them how to speak to themself in a kind and caring way, especially when they are going through a difficult time. The worksheet is available for download in color from http://www .newharbinger.com/49760.

Worksheet 7: The Kind and Caring Coach

Imagine a very kind and caring coach, who told you that you were trying really hard and doing a great job. Now draw a coach below, and write down some really kind and caring things this coach might say to you when it's hard for you to cope with your thoughts and feelings (for example, when you feel sad, worried, scared, angry, or something else). Then you can practice saying those kind and caring things to yourself.

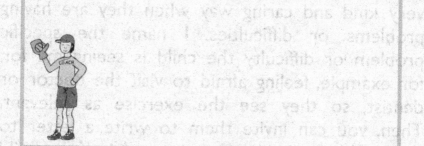

Write a Kind and Caring Letter to Yourself

I find that children respond well to this exercise, which I adapted from Russell Kolts's

(2016) Compassionate Letter-Writing. In my experience, both young children as well as older children who are very self-critical are usually able to come up with some kind and caring language once they start writing themselves a letter. Sometimes, children who are very self-critical will surprise you by writing themselves quite long kind and caring letters. I've had children tell me after writing themselves a kind and caring letter that they found it helpful and enjoyed writing it. By writing themselves a letter, children experience *how* to speak to themselves in a kind and caring way, which is especially powerful for children who might initially struggle with coming up with kind and caring language to use toward themselves.

The instructions for this exercise are as follows: Give the child a sheet of paper and some pencils or a pen, and ask them to think about how they might speak to themself in a very kind and caring way when they are having problems or difficulties. I name the specific problem or difficulty the child is seeing me for, for example, feeling afraid to visit the doctor or dentist, so they see the exercise as relevant. Then, you can invite them to write a letter to themself, using kind and caring words. If the child is in their first few years of school, or you know they have writing or spelling difficulties, ask if they would prefer to say their letter aloud and you will write what they say.

The following is an example of how I would introduce this exercise to a child who is afraid of going into a doctor's or dentist's office. Feel free to adapt this script in any way you like:

Think about a time when you arrived at the doctor's or dentist's office and felt afraid to walk inside. If any thoughts of not being able to do this show up, such as "I'm scared to walk into the doctor's or dentist's office," or "I can't do this," that's okay, just let those thoughts be, without trying to do anything with them. (This is a reminder of or introduction to the ACT Kidflex process let it be.) Now, think about how you might speak to yourself in an especially kind and caring way about feeling afraid to walk into the doctor's or dentist's office. Imagine that you use a kind, caring, and calm voice to speak to yourself; try to imagine what your voice would sound like. Think about what you could say to yourself as a reminder that you've felt afraid in the past to walk into the doctor's or dentist's office, and you've gotten yourself through it—you were okay. You walked into the office, even though your mind told you that you were afraid. (The phrase "your mind told you" is a reminder of or introduction to the ACT Kidflex process let it go. Pause, allowing the child a few minutes to consider this.)

Now, I'd like to invite you to try writing a kind and caring letter to yourself. You might like to start with something like "Dear (insert the child's name), I know that walking into the doctor's or dentist's office is really hard for you. You will be safe walking into the office, and I will be here for you. You've gotten yourself through times when you felt afraid before." There is no right or wrong way to write this. I won't be correcting your letter, and when you finish, I won't read it unless you want me to. Whatever you write will be just fine.

If the child writes a few words, then stops and says they don't know what else to write, you could suggest that they think about someone who is very kind and caring (perhaps someone they know, such as a family member, friend, teacher, or pet, or perhaps a character in a book, television show, or movie; Bluth, 2017) and what they might say to them if they knew they were afraid of walking into the doctor's or dentist's office. You can encourage the child to think about what kind and caring words that person might say to them, and then they can write that down.

After the child has finished writing, ask if they would like you to read the letter back to them, reassuring them that they don't have to agree, and letting them know that you won't be upset or disappointed if they don't agree. This may help alleviate any pressure that the child may feel to agree. If the child agrees to your reading the letter, read it aloud slowly, pausing so that the child *really* listens to the words. Then, ask if there are any other situations where it might be helpful to write a kind and caring letter and then read it to themself. Ask if they would like to take their letter home, and if they do, you might like to suggest that they put the letter on the wall in their bedroom or in a safe place and read it when they are going through a difficult time, or when they notice that they are not being kind and caring to themself. (The phrase "when you notice" reminds the child of or introduces them to the ACT Kidflex process *notice yourself*. For more detail, see chapter 5.) I've had children tell me a few weeks after writing this letter that they've been reading it at home and have found it helpful.

Imagine a Kind and Caring Friend

This exercise is helpful for children who struggle to think of kind and caring ways to speak to themselves. I use this exercise a lot, and find that it works very well with children aged five to twelve years. In my experience, children who feel very connected to their pet often choose to imagine their pet instead of a person. If you know that the child is very connected to their pet, ask the child the pet's name if you don't already know it. Then, when you suggest to the child that they imagine a friend, family member, teacher, or pet, you can refer to their pet by name. The following script is adapted from Bluth's (2017) and Neff and Germer's (2018) Compassionate Friend meditation; feel free to adapt it further in any way:

> For this exercise, you can close your eyes, or keep them open. If you prefer to keep your eyes open, I recommend that you focus on a spot on the floor, in order to concentrate. Imagine a safe place, where you feel relaxed and peaceful, like a beach or forest, or somewhere else. Imagine that a kind and caring friend, or family member, or teacher, or pet visits you there. Imagine they're sitting next to you, and that they understand what life is like for you, and what's difficult for you. Imagine they say something kind and caring to you, and if you want to, you can say something back to them. Take a few minutes to notice this person or pet, notice yourself, and notice how you're feeling. Let your thoughts and feelings be, without trying to do anything with them. (Pause here, allowing the child a few minutes for this.)
>
> If your attention drifts away, and you notice yourself thinking about other things, gently bring your attention back to imagining a safe place, and someone visiting you there. Then, say goodbye to them. It's okay; you can come back to this safe place and invite them to come back another time. When you're ready, open your eyes and come back to being here in the room (or online) with me.

You might have noticed that I included some of the ACT Kidflex processes. The phrases "notice yourself" and "notice how you're feeling" remind the child of or introduce them to the *notice yourself* process, and "let your thoughts and feelings be, without trying to do anything with them" reminds the child of or introduces them to the *let it be* process. The statement "If your attention drifts away, and you notice yourself thinking about other things, gently bring your attention back" reminds the child of or introduces them to the *stay here* process, which shows the child how to combine those processes with *be kind and caring to yourself.*

After allowing the child a few minutes to get used to being back in the room (or online) with you, ask if they would like to tell you what it was like trying to imagine visiting with a kind and caring friend.

HELPFUL HINT

As a reminder, I don't ask children how they "found exercises," as they may take you literally and reply that they didn't find it; you did. This is something to keep in mind particularly with autistic children.

If they don't wish to discuss the exercise, you can reassure them that it's okay, they don't have to. If they would like to, you could ask some or all of the following questions:

- "Where did you imagine you were?"
- "Who was there with you?"
- "Would you like to share what the person (or pet) said to you?" Again, reassure them that they don't have to tell you if they don't wish to. If the child tells you, you can ask, "Would you like to share what you replied to the person (or pet)?"
- "What was it like saying goodbye to the person (or pet)?"
- "Do you think it might be helpful to try this exercise on your own, perhaps at home, or school, or somewhere else?" If the child isn't sure, you could provide some suggestions, based on the problem or difficulty the child is seeing you for. For example, you could suggest that when their mind tells them they are anxious about presenting in class (the phrase "when your mind tells you" reminds them of or introduces them to the ACT Kidflex process *let it go*), they could think about what a kind and caring person/family member/friend/teacher/pet might say to them.
- "Is there anything that might make it difficult to try this exercise on your own?"
- "What might help you to remember to practice speaking to yourself in a kind and caring way?"

Let's look now at how you can use chair work with children.

Chair Work

Chair work refers to a group of experiential techniques that involve positioning several chairs and moving the client between the chairs (Bell et al., 2019). It has been used extensively for addressing self-criticism as part of emotion-focused therapy (Greenberg et al., 1993; Greenberg & Watson, 2006) and schema therapy (Rafaeli et al., 2011; Roediger et al., 2018). Although chair work was designed for use with adults, I find that it can also be used effectively with children. Below I'll describe two versions of chair work.

The Empty Chair

I adapted this exercise from Russell Kolts (2016). In my experience, this exercise works really well with children aged seven to twelve years old. (If you'd like to try use it with five- to six-year-old children, you could see how it goes. If you find that it isn't suitable, you could use either the Write a Kind and Caring Letter exercise or Imagine a Kind and Caring Friend exercise provided earlier in this chapter instead.) For this exercise, I place a chair next to the child, facing the same direction as the chair the child is seated on. Although when doing empty-chair work with adults, most therapists place the chair opposite the client, my own preference is to position the empty chair next to the child, as I feel this is less confronting and intimidating, which may help the child feel more comfortable—and then be more willing to participate in this exercise. If you prefer to place the empty chair opposite the child instead of next to them, feel free to do so. If the child is uncomfortable or resistant, you could then move the chair next to them and see if they are more comfortable or willing.

Let's look now at a transcript of how I used the empty-chair exercise with eight-year-old Lola (see chapter 5 for a reminder about Lola). Feel free to adapt this in any way to use with your clients:

Therapist: Lola, I'd like to invite you to participate in an activity where you imagine that someone is sitting in the chair next to you. This is someone who really cares about you, who only ever wants the best for you, and always encourages and reassures you. Would you be willing to try this exercise?

Lola: Sure.

Therapist: That's great, thank you. This person only ever uses kind and caring words when they speak to you. They are *never* mean to you or critical of you. This might be someone who's in your life now, or someone who was in your life in the past. If you haven't had anyone like that in your life, I'd like you to try to imagine what such a person would be like. *(I paused, allowing Lola to think about this.)* Is there someone like this that you could imagine sitting here with us?

Lola: My best friend Jenny. She's one of the kindest people I know. She's always there for me, and she's super lovely. She's been my best friend since I started elementary school.

Therapist: I'd like you to imagine that Jenny has been sitting here with us, listening carefully to every word you said, and *really* noticing what a hard time you've been giving yourself, and how you have been being very mean to yourself. She listened as you criticized your dance skills and said that you have to dance perfectly and not make any mistakes. What do you think Jenny might say if she was sitting in the room with us? What advice might Jenny give you?

Lola: She'd be annoyed with me for being so mean to myself. She's always telling me I'm a great dancer and that I should be kinder to myself and be proud of my skills.

Therapist: If Jenny were to give you some suggestions for how you could speak to yourself in a really kind and caring way, what would she say?

Lola: She'd say that I'm too hard on myself, and that I should remind myself how hard I practice. Jenny would say that I'm really brave for performing on stage in front of an audience, because she hates being on stage! The day before my concerts, she always tells me that the most important thing is to have fun. She says to me, "Don't sweat the small stuff," which means that I shouldn't get upset or annoyed about little things, that probably aren't really important.

Therapist: What would Jenny say about how you think your teacher would feel if you didn't dance perfectly?

Lola: Jenny would say that my teacher would be so proud of me because she knows how hard

I trained all year, and that I deserve to treat myself better.

Therapist: You did that exercise really well Lola. What do you think of what Jenny said to you? Did she get it correct?

Lola: I think she's correct, and maybe I need to try speaking to myself more like Jenny speaks to me.

At the end of this exercise, you could ask the child to think about other situations where it might be helpful to imagine someone sitting next to them who only ever speaks to them in a kind and caring way, and what that person would say if they heard the child giving themself a hard time. You could suggest that the next time they notice themself (this reminds them of or introduces them to the ACT Kidflex process *notice yourself*) using unkind words to speak to themself, they could try to imagine that the kind and caring person is sitting next to them, giving them suggestions about how they could speak to themself in a kinder and more caring way.

Using the Empty Chair to Give a Friend Advice

I adapted this exercise from Kristen Neff and Christopher Germer's (2018) How Do I Treat a Friend exercise. Sometimes, I first try the Empty Chair exercise described above, but if the child is unable to or doesn't want to imagine someone kind and caring (particularly if they've never had anyone in their life like this), you can do this alternative exercise in which you ask the child what they'd tell a friend (or family member or pet) who had a problem or difficulty.

I also recommend trying this exercise instead of the Empty Chair exercise above if you know that the child is very rigid in their thinking (for example, has great difficulty considering alternative ways to do things, or argues when you give them suggestions for how they could do things differently). This is because some children find it easier to consider how *others* would approach problems and difficulties than to think about what advice someone else would give them.

In short, this exercise involves having the child imagine that a friend is sitting in the chair next to them and is telling them about a problem or difficulty they are having, and then asking the child to give their friend suggestions for how they might help themself (in a sense, the reverse of the Empty Chair exercise above). Below we'll review a case example that illustrates, in more detail, the use of this exercise.

HELPFUL HINT

You might like to use both versions of the Empty Chair exercise with the same child, or you can choose the exercise that you think will be best suited to the child.

Case Example: Mateo, Nine Years Old

Mateo's parents had separated, and he struggled to cope with the changes associated with this, such as moving back and forth between two homes and having to decide what to pack each time. He blamed himself for his parents' breakup and was very self-critical. Let's look now at a transcript of how the exercise Using the Empty Chair to Give a Friend Advice went with Mateo:

Therapist: I'd like to invite you to participate in an exercise now where you imagine that a friend is sitting in the chair next to you, and telling us about a problem or difficulty of their own. Then I'll ask you to give them some suggestions for how they might help themself. Would you like to try this exercise?

Mateo: Sure!

Therapist: Great, thank you. Could you tell me the first name of the friend you'd like to imagine is sitting next to you?

Mateo: Alex—they're my best friend.

Therapist: I'd like you to try to pretend that Alex is sitting here with us, and has been telling you that they have a basketball competition coming up, which they are super worried about. Alex has been telling themself that they better score plenty of points for their team, otherwise the team will be really disappointed with them. Could you give Alex some suggestions for how they could speak to themself in a more kind and caring way?

Mateo: Definitely. Alex, you're really, really good at basketball. You train so hard, and always play really well. But even if you *don't* play well in the next game, that doesn't matter at all, because all that's really important is that you give it your best shot. No one can ask any more from you than that.

Therapist: Could you also try to tell Alex what they might be able to try when they notice that they're being unkind to themself? (*The phrase "notice that they're being unkind to themself" reminds or introduces Mateo to the ACT Kidflex notice yourself process. This teaches Mateo how to combine be kind* and caring to yourself *with the* notice yourself *process.)*

Mateo: Alex, your basketball team is lucky to have you on the team, and you're always such a good sport, even cheering for the other team when they do well and congratulating them when they win. You try super hard, and you're so kind to everyone on the team, always taking care to try to make them feel better if they don't play well. No matter how you play, I'll always be proud of you, and proud to call you my best friend. You're caring, kind, and the nicest person I know.

Therapist: Wow Mateo, you've been very kind and caring to Alex, and have given them some great suggestions. Well done!

Mateo: Thank you.

Therapist: Mateo, do you think that how Alex treats themself and speaks to themself is helping them and working for them?

Mateo: Definitely not.

Therapist: Was it easy to think of how Alex could speak to themself in a more kind and caring way, or was it hard?

Mateo: It was easy. Alex was being mean to themself, and what they were saying about themself wasn't the truth.

Therapist: Were there any differences in the way that you spoke to Alex from how you speak to yourself?

Mateo: Yes, I think I'm *much* nicer to Alex than I am to myself, because it's easy to be nice to them, but sometimes it's *really* hard to be nice to myself, especially if I think I've messed up.

Therapist: Mateo, which way do you think would work better for speaking to *yourself:* the kind, caring, and really supportive way that you spoke to Alex, or the very critical way that you speak to yourself, where you put lots of pressure on yourself?

Mateo: Umm, I think the way I spoke to Alex. When I spoke to Alex in a very kind way, it made them happy, and they looked calmer, but when I'm mean to myself I get even sadder, and worry about messing up.

Therapist: When you start to notice yourself speaking to yourself in a mean or unkind way, you might like to stop for a moment, and notice where you are, and what's happening around you. Then, you can think about the kind and caring way that you spoke to Alex here today, and try saying some of those words to yourself. *(Using the phrase "notice yourself" here again teaches Mateo how to combine be kind and caring to yourself with the ACT Kidflex notice yourself process, and "notice where you are, and what's happening around you" reminds or introduces Mateo to the ACT Kidflex stay here process.)*

Mateo: That'll be *very* different, but I'm happy to try it.

Therapist: That's great; you did really well with this exercise. I know it's not easy, and you deserve to be very proud of yourself for giving it a go.

Mateo: Thank you.

As we've discussed, parents can also play a big role in encouraging their children to implement the ACT Kidflex processes in their lives. Let's look now at suggestions you can give to parents to help their child be kind and caring to themself.

Suggestions for Parents

One of the most important suggestions I give to parents is that they model using kind and caring self-talk in front of the child. I recommend that parents do this for neutral, everyday situations. For example, the parent can say aloud, "I'm finding that learning how to do this task is *really* difficult, but I'm trying my best. Nothing bad is going to happen if I can't figure out how to do this, and if I need to ask for help, that's okay."

I also suggest that parents use kind and caring language to coach their child when the child is experiencing a problem or difficulty. For example, if the child is afraid before getting a shot, the parent can reassure them that they know how hard getting a shot is for them, that they have everything they need to get through this, and that feeling afraid won't last forever.

When the child is struggling to cope, parents can also ask the child, "If a friend of yours was going through this, or going through something similar, what could you say that might be helpful for them?" In addition, I suggest to parents that they model to the child what they *themself* might tell a friend that may be helpful for the friend.

If the parent is experiencing a problem or difficulty of their own, they can model using this same strategy for themself. (You can remind the parent gently that any self-disclosure should be appropriate for the child to hear and should not cause the child to worry about their parent.) The parent can say something to the child like "I'm sure if I told my good friend Ashley that I'm feeling nervous about starting my new job, Ashley would tell me that anyone would be nervous about changing jobs, and that I should be proud of myself for getting the new job."

Finally, you can recommend to parents that when their child is struggling with a problem or difficulty, they encourage their child to do some of the exercises at home that you have done with their child in therapy sessions (such as Write a Kind and Caring Letter to Yourself, or Imagine a Kind and Caring Friend). The parent could ask their child what they would tell a friend who was having the same problem or difficulty, or they could suggest that the child imagine what a kind and caring friend, family member, or pet would tell them. The parent could also remind the child of The Two Coaches exercise, and ask the child how a kind and caring coach would speak to the child about their problem or difficulty, and what that coach might suggest.

Conclusion

In this session, you have introduced the child to *be kind and caring to yourself* to teach them how to help themself when they are self-critical, have unrealistic expectations of themself, put a lot of pressure on themself, or are giving themself a hard time. You have given them language they can use to coach themself through problems and difficulties, and you've also shown them how to acknowledge and praise themself when they are coping with challenges.

You have also shown the child how they can use this together with some of the ACT Kidflex processes. If you completed addressing the processes in the ACT Kidflex before introducing the child to *be kind and caring to yourself*, this session will have taught them how to use *be kind and caring to yourself* together with what they've already learned about ACT. If you haven't taught them all the processes of the ACT Kidflex yet, this session may have been an introduction to some of the processes, through learning some phrases they can use based on ACT Kidflex processes.

The child will now have a better understanding of what being kind and caring to themself means, and they may have realized for the first time that the way they speak to others is far more kind and caring than how they speak to themself. This may help them notice when they are being unkind and uncaring to themself, and they may use some of the exercises in this chapter to help change their self-talk and practice being kinder and more caring to themself. These tools will likely increase the child's faith in their own ability to manage their difficulties for a wide range of situations and to self-soothe, perhaps resulting in reduced levels of distress for future problems and difficulties.

This chapter also provided simple recommendations you can provide to parents, including modeling *be kind and caring to yourself* at home, reminding the child and reinforcing what they've learned in therapy sessions, and helping their child be kinder and more caring to themself when they are experiencing problems and difficulties.

Be kind and caring to yourself complements all the processes of the ACT Kidflex *(let it be, let it go, choose what matters, do what matters, stay here,* and *notice yourself)*, equipping the child not only to manage the problem or difficulty they presented to you for help with, but also with skills for life, thereby increasing their resilience. With regular practice over time, they will become more proficient and skilled in these techniques, which may become core components of their coping toolkit. To read a session-by-session description of how I implemented the ACT Kidflex and *be kind and caring to yourself* with an eight-year-old child, go to http://www.newharbin ger.com/49760. In the next chapter, we'll focus on working with parents without treating their child.

CHAPTER 7

When Parents Are the Client

In the previous chapter, we read about teaching children to be kind and caring to themselves and become their own coaches, instead of engaging in self-criticism. We'll shift our focus in this chapter from working with the child to providing therapy to parents of young children when you haven't been able to engage the child. We'll look at training parents in how to use the ACT Kidflex and *be kind and caring to yourself* so they can model the processes to their child and also directly teach their child how to deal with their thoughts and feelings in order to cope better with their problem or difficulty. This chapter will include how to use exercises with parents in sessions as part of teaching them how to help their child, along with recommended home tasks for parents to practice in the presence of and together with their child. All exercises in this chapter can be used in session with one or more parents.

Determining When to Work with the Parent Alone

Sometimes, you may find yourself working with a child who is particularly hard to engage. You have tried your absolute best and use the most creative methods you can think of, like inviting the child to join you in some of the exercises we discussed in chapters 3 through 5. The reality is that there are some children who simply don't want to participate in therapy sessions, and nothing you do will change their mind.

When this occurs (and it *will* occur with some children—which is *not* a negative reflection of you as a therapist), I find it helpful to stop for a minute and press my own imaginary "pause button," rather than coming up with even more ideas to try to engage the child. I notice what thoughts are showing up in my own mind (which are very likely to be self-critical, and something like *If only you were better at this, this would never happen,* or *I bet you are the only ACT therapist this happens to!* or *You are a really lousy child psychologist).* I let those thoughts be: by noticing what I'm feeling in my body and where it's showing up, just sitting with what's happening in my mind and in the therapy room, and thanking my mind for the thought. I can let go of the thought that I have to succeed at engaging the child today, by saying something to myself like

There's my mind, having the thought that I have to succeed at engaging this child today.

When this occurs, use some of the ACT processes you've learned in this book to help you manage this moment (such as *let it be* and *let it go*), and then move forward, knowing that there's someone else you might be able to work with: the parent. When I work with children aged five to twelve years, I ask that the parent attend the first session together with their child to give their input when I conduct a case conceptualization (see chapter 2 for more detail) and to provide the child's history. Observing what's happening between the child and their parent during the first session is often very representative of how they interact with each other in day-to-day life. This enables you to gather data about the power balance between them and the way the parent responds to their child. For example, you might notice the parent becoming very anxious when their child doesn't answer your questions and doesn't participate in exercises, and they may even offer their child a reward in exchange for cooperating. This might lead the child to expect a reward for cooperating in other environments, such as at school or in team sports.

If you see this occur, think about whether you might be able to help the parent by seeing them for therapy on their own, then make a note of possible treatment goals. Goals could include teaching them strategies to help their child manage their thoughts and feelings about participating in activities they don't want to do, or are afraid or anxious to do, and teaching the parent to be kind and caring to themself, so that they don't blame themself when their child doesn't respond to their attempts to manage their behavior.

Engaging Parents in Therapy

When you are unable to engage a child after a couple of sessions, and you feel it might be helpful to provide therapy to the parent (or parents) instead, particularly if the child is younger, say five to eight years, I recommend acknowledging to the parent that you're unable to engage the child and are unsure of what else to try. It's important to keep in mind that if the child is disengaged, the parent might feel very anxious and be worried that you will judge them as a result of their child's refusal to take part.

HELPFUL HINT

Reassure the parent that it's okay that the child doesn't want to participate, and that it's not a reflection of the parent in any way. If you can't engage the child, suggest to the parent that you could work with them instead of the child, to give the parent strategies they can teach their child.

Consider asking the parent if they would they like to see you for therapy themself to address the problems or difficulties their child is experiencing. Let them know that you will train them in the ACT Kidflex and in *be kind and caring to yourself*: this will include how to model and teach their child strategies to help regulate their emotions. You can explain to the parent that through your work together, they'll be able to help the child learn new and more effective ways to cope with their thoughts and feelings, become less overwhelmed, and self-soothe, which may lead to the child becoming more resilient.

To illustrate how to approach the suggestion of working with parents without their child, we'll look at an example.

Case Example: Allie, Five Years Old

Mary and Andres brought their daughter, Allie, to see me for therapy because of significant problems she was experiencing as a result of separation anxiety. Allie has two sisters, seven-year-old Samantha and two-year-old Kerry. I saw Allie together with her parents for two sessions, but was unsuccessful in engaging Allie. In response, I invited Mary and Andres to participate in sessions with me instead of my treating Allie, which they agreed to.

Let's look at how I suggested this to Mary and Andres:

Therapist: I'm finding it really hard to engage Allie; we've tried two sessions now, where I invited her to participate in drawing, art, and blowing bubbles, but she's made it clear that she *really* doesn't want to be here, and isn't going to take part in anything I suggest.

Andres: I'm really sorry, I had hoped that once she came and met you a couple of times she'd be willing to talk about what worries her at preschool.

Therapist: That's okay; it's not your fault Allie doesn't want to take part. Sometimes this happens—she might not feel that she needs to be here.

Mary: Allie's supposed to start elementary school in three months, but her preschool teachers have just told us they don't think she's ready because she gets so distressed upon arrival at preschool.

Therapist: Allie might feel that things are perfectly fine the way they are and that she doesn't need any help. This is really common, and isn't anyone's fault. If she decides in the future that she does want help with being able to separate from you, you could let her know that she can see me again, and if she agrees, you can return. But Allie might not reach that decision for a really long time, and I've heard from you today how distressed she gets when you drop her off at preschool. Allie must be really struggling with her thoughts and feelings, and become overwhelmed, which might not help her self-esteem, or help her cope with other challenges. It might also be detrimental to her friendships with the other children at preschool.

Mary: Allie's teachers won't give her approval to start elementary school unless she gets some help. She'd be devastated if we told her that she can't start school with her friends.

Andres: Our older daughter, Samantha, is already at school, and when we take Allie to the school to pick up Samantha, they play in the playground together. Allie's expecting to start school in a few months.

Therapist: I'm hearing that it's really important to you that Allie start school in a few months with her friends, and it sounds like you both feel that things would be worse for Allie if she does another year of preschool.

Andres: Definitely!

Mary: I agree.

Therapist: In that case, I want to suggest that you both see me for therapy instead. In our sessions, I'll invite you to take part in some exercises that will teach you about ACT (*I had already explained to them in the first session what ACT is*), and I'll also train you to teach ACT to Allie, using some different strategies from the ones you've been using. I'll teach you how you can show Allie how to use the strategies herself to cope with feeling anxious. As a result, she'll learn how she can join the other children quickly when she arrives at preschool, and also learn how to manage her thoughts and feelings herself, which may help increase her self-esteem. I think this might help you to get Allie ready to start school in three months.

Mary: That would be wonderful, thank you.

Andres: Great, let's do it. And if there's anything we're doing as parents that you don't think we should be doing, or if you think there's room for improvement, please just tell us—we're open to hearing anything you think could help Allie.

Therapist: That's great, thank you. I'd love to work with you both to try to help Allie, and thank you for being so willing to hear some new ideas and approaches.

Rather than discussing how the parents can get their child to attend therapy, I ask the parents if they are willing to learn some strategies to help their child. In the transcript with Mary and Andres above, I modeled *be kind and caring to yourself,* by letting them know that it wasn't their fault that Allie didn't want to participate in therapy. I also acknowledged that this can happen when trying to engage children in therapy, which teaches Mary and Andres to use be *kind and caring to yourself.* The reason I did this was so that Mary and Andres wouldn't blame themselves for Allie's reluctance and to let them know that it's okay if Allie doesn't want to attend therapy.

When using ACT with clients—whether individual adults, or parents and children—we don't try to convince them that we can help, or that ACT is really great. As such, I let Mary and Andres know that I'd like to work with them to *try* to help Allie. I also thanked Andres for his and Mary's willingness to hear some new approaches; this was to positively reinforce their flexibility, which is consistent with the aim of the ACT Kidflex: *I am flexible.*

We'll return to Mary and Andres later in this chapter. For now, though, let's look at exercises you can use in sessions with parents.

Exercises to Use with Parents

Many of the exercises for children in chapters 3 through 6 can also be used with one or more parents in therapy sessions (you can change the scenario to something more adult-oriented as appropriate). These exercises are outlined in table 1. I'll also show you some other exercises suitable for use with parents that we haven't yet looked at.

TABLE 1. ACT Kidflex and Be Kind and Caring to Yourself Exercises Suitable for Parents

Process	Exercise	Ch
Let It Be	Don't Think About Chocolate Cake Saying Hello to Our Thoughts and Feelings	3
Let It Go	I'm Having the Thought That Naming the Story Thanking Your Mind Waves on the Ocean	3
Choose What Matters	Write a "Thank You for Being You" Card What's in My Heart (use the Parenting Bull's-Eye version outlined below)	4
Stay Here	Staying Here and Being Elsewhere Eating While Staying Here Listening to Music While Staying Here	5
Notice Yourself	Still Quiet Ship The Beach Under the Sea Watching a Movie of Your Life (or Your Family)	5
Be Kind and Caring to Yourself	The Two Coaches Write a Kind and Caring Letter to Yourself Imagine a Kind and Caring Friend The Empty Chair	6

Note: You may have noticed that *do what matters* isn't listed in table 1. As a reminder, instead of consisting of exercises in therapy sessions, *do what matters* includes actions such as attending therapy sessions, participating in exercises, completing home tasks suggested in therapy sessions, and starting to do the things that matter based on *choose what matters* (see chapter 4 for more detail).

Let's look now at some other exercises that you can use with parents during therapy sessions to teach them the ACT Kidflex processes and *be kind and caring to yourself.*

Let It Be and Let It Go for Parents

Teaching parents the ACT Kidflex processes *let it be* and *let it go* is a useful way to help them support their child. And a valuable by-product of this can be that you actually increase the parents' *own* flexibility (remember, the goal of the ACT Kidflex is *I am flexible*), which may in turn help their child. By teaching parents about *let it be* and *let it go* and how to teach and model these processes to their child, their child might then be able to start regulating and managing their own emotions.

Before you start teaching parents how to use the ACT Kidflex processes *let it be* and *let it go* with their child, I find it helpful to take parents through the processes first so that they can experience the processes for themselves. I recommend that you give parents an example they're likely to relate to, as this often makes it easier for parents to understand the concepts quickly. It's often helpful to use an example of parents blaming themselves for their child's problem or difficulty, as thoughts and feelings of self-blame are common for parents.

From Then to Now

I adapted this exercise from Coyne and Murrell's (2009) A Look Back exercise. You can use the script below, or adapt it to fit the case:

Think about one early memory of your child from when they were younger, and notice where your child was, who else was present, and what your child was doing. Try to pay attention to how it feels to recall that memory, and just notice whatever thoughts are showing up. Now think of a recent memory of your child, perhaps of your child struggling to cope with their problem or difficulty, and watch how they react when they struggle with their thoughts and feelings.

Think about what might have changed from then to now, and whether things are different now from how they used to be. Perhaps you or your child started using different or new strategies to try to cope with problems or difficulties. As you think of these memories, and why your child's behavior or worries might have changed, or worsened, allow whatever images, thoughts, and feelings that show up in your mind to just be there. Notice how that feels, just letting it be, without trying to do *anything. If you start to notice yourself blaming yourself for your child's problem or difficulty, you can use the phrase "I'm having the thought that it's all my fault," followed by "Thanks mind" (this not only teaches parents how to use the let it be and let it go processes, but also teaches them the notice yourself process).*

After parents experience *let it be* and *let it go* for themselves, you can teach them how to introduce *let it be* and *let it go* with their child, using a specific scenario, problem, or difficulty the parents have mentioned to you previously. Let's say they are moving to a new house, and the child is very anxious and upset. You might say something like this to the parent:

When you notice that your child is worried, sad, angry, or having a meltdown, or when they tell you how they're feeling, you can encourage them to let their thoughts and feelings be, and let their thoughts and feelings go. You could say something to your child like "I understand that you're worried about moving to a new house. You can notice the thoughts that your mind is coming up with, allowing them to be there, without trying to do anything to get rid of them. You can notice how that feels, and let those thoughts be, without trying to do anything with them. When you have a thought about being worried about moving to a new house, you can try saying, 'I'm having the thought that

I'm worried about moving to a new house';
then you can say, 'Thanks mind for that
interesting thought.'

HELPFUL HINT

When giving parents suggestions for specific
things they can say to help their child, I
recommend offering to write the suggestions
on paper (in face-to-face sessions) or via email
in online sessions, so parents don't have to
try to remember what you've said. Some
parents may respond by typing the suggestions
in their phone, or may ask you for paper and
pen, or may take you up on your offer to
write out or email the suggestions.

Be Kind and Caring to Yourself for Parents

Just as for children who are learning about
be kind and caring to yourself, it's often helpful for
parents to write a letter to themselves to learn
this skill. Then, parents will be able to teach
their child how they can use kind and caring
language when the child is distressed, and they
can also suggest that the child practice speaking
to themselves using kind and caring language each
day, so this becomes part of the child's regular
self-talk. This is a useful exercise to do early in
your work with parents, and it helps to set the

tone for parents who may tend to be self-critical or self-blaming regarding their parenting.

Write a Letter to Yourself

I adapted this exercise from Coyne and Murrell's (2009) A Letter to Your Child exercise. For this exercise, you can invite parents to write themselves a letter about what matters most to them (choose what matters) about being a parent. (If you are working with two parents, I recommend inviting them each to write a letter to themself.) They can also include their hopes and dreams: for their child, for how they want to parent their child, and also for their relationship with their child. You can invite them to write about a specific time when they felt that how they parented their child worked well, and what actions they did that were most helpful. Then, they can write about what actions they could try to do more of in order to help their child, followed by what actions they do that they don't feel are helpful for their child. Doing this will help equip parents to have a conversation with their child about what actions the child is doing that might not be helpful for them.

You can suggest that parents try to include some kind and caring statements about themselves as parents in their letter (be kind and caring to yourself), for example, "I'm trying my best," "Parenting is the hardest job I've ever had; it's okay that I don't always know the best way to help my child," and "I'm doing a really good job supporting my child through a very tough phase in their life." You can also suggest that they consider including some actions they could do to be kinder and more caring toward themselves.

After they've finished writing, you might like to invite parents to share their letter with you, letting them know that they don't have to. I recommend suggesting that they take their letter home and look at it when they notice they are giving themselves a hard time about being a parent (this also uses the *notice yourself* process), which might remind them how hard they are trying to care for and help their child. If they wish to take the letter home, you might like to ask their permission to photograph or photocopy their work for your file.

Depending on the age of the child (as a general rule, I wouldn't suggest this for children under the age of six), you can suggest to parents that they help their child write a kind and caring letter to themself (see Write a Kind and Caring Letter to Yourself, chapter 6). Let the parent know that the child might need their help with some examples of kind and caring words they could include, in order to help them get started. The parent can suggest that the child keep the letter in a safe place, and that when they are distressed, they read the letter, or the parent can offer to read the letter to the child.

Do What Matters for Parents

When parents remain focused on what matters to them and continue working toward what matters, they are better able to remain consistent in supporting their child. The following exercise helps parents to identify what matters most to them.

Parenting Bull's-Eye

This *do what matters* exercise is similar to the What's in My Heart exercise for children (see chapter 4 for more details), which I adapted from Dahl and Lundgren's Bull's-Eye (2006). Give the parent a piece of paper (or one each if there are two parents in attendance) and invite them to draw a circle. Then ask them to think about how the child copes with their problem or difficulty, and choose one thing that matters to them (as parents) that they could do to try to help their child cope. Then they can write that in the middle of the circle. Invite the parent to consider how close or how far away they are from doing that thing that matters to help their child, and ask them to draw a dot somewhere in the circle representing this.

It's helpful to give them an example, for example, perhaps they would like their child to be able to fall asleep on their own, but when their child cries at bedtime, they sit on their child's bed until they fall asleep. If the child's falling asleep on their own is something that matters to the parent, they could write that, then they could consider whether sitting on their child's bed until the child falls asleep actually helps their child to learn to regulate their own emotions and let their anxiety be (*let it be*). You can explain that if they do walk out of their child's room after saying goodnight, they would draw a dot close to the middle of the circle, but if they stay in their child's room until the child falls asleep, then they would draw the dot far away.

I recommend explaining to the parent that you are asking about whether they actually *do* the thing that matters to them (for example, allow the child to fall asleep on their own), and if so, it might help to think about whether they do this often, infrequently, or never. Then, you can invite the parent to share what they've written with you (and with each other if there are two parents in attendance).

After this, ask the parent if there's anything that might make it difficult to do the action they've written. For example, if their child screams or cries when they leave the room, the parent might return to the room and remain there until the child falls asleep because they don't want their child to be distressed, and because they may feel guilty about having upset their child.

Anticipating possible outcomes and helping the parent plan for these can be very helpful in preventing the parent from becoming distressed, anxious, or overwhelmed by their child's reaction, and then becoming unsure of how to respond. It also establishes a greater likelihood of the parent's responding consistently and doing what matters. This is particularly important if the child lives with two parents who respond in contradictory ways—such as one walking out of the child's room before the child falls asleep, only for the other parent to go in and remain with the child until they fall asleep.

Stay Here and Notice Yourself for Parents

As we learned in chapter 5, the ACT Kidflex process *stay here* refers to being present and aware of your experiences, and *notice yourself* refers to standing back and watching yourself. When applying these processes to adults, they can be used as part of teaching self-care.

Self-care is highly important for parents and is also a critical skill to teach and model to their children. By engaging in regular self-care, parents are less likely to experience burnout and perhaps illness too. When parents incorporate their own self-care, they are often better able to offer attentive care to their children. The following exercise is a helpful way for parents to develop a self-care plan.

Planning Your Self-Care

This exercise is an adaptation of Worksheet 5: Staying Here, where children are invited to make a list of activities they can do to practice staying here and really noticing what's happening around them, instead of being caught up in their thoughts (see chapter 5 for more detail). It also addresses the *notice yourself* process.

I begin by inviting parents to think about how they could schedule their own regular self-care, using their day-to-day activities, instead of trying to add more to what's often a very busy schedule, especially if they are the sole parent. If needed, I give them suggestions from the *stay here* exercises for home practice in chapter 5—like listening to music, painting or drawing, and reading—which parents can do on their own as part of regular parent self-care. Parents might also benefit from quiet time, cooking themselves a favorite meal (rather than only preparing meals their children enjoy), meditating, or mindfully stretching before going to bed as a way of letting go of the stress and busyness of the day. Many parents practice self-care infrequently due to time constraints and, in some cases, fatigue. This exercise is a way for them to identify activities they can incorporate into their regular routine without requiring excessive time.

I encourage parents to practice staying here and trying to notice themselves while engaging in self-care. Staying here and noticing themselves helps parents remember to focus on themselves, which is something many parents don't prioritize but is important for their own well-being. As a result of the benefits they receive from their own self-care, parents will also be better able to support and help their child. Parents can also encourage their child to practice their own self-care by asking them to think of some activities they could do. They can also suggest some activities to the child, for example, reading, drawing, or listening to music.

Let's return to the example of Mary and Andres, parents of five-year-old Allie. They attended therapy for six sessions in total: the first two sessions with Allie, then another four sessions without Allie.

Case Example: Mary and Andres

As you'll recall, Allie had refused to answer my questions and wouldn't participate in any exercises, so instead of treating Allie, I worked with Mary and Andres directly to help them prepare Allie to start elementary school. Mary and Andres reported that Allie had always been "clingy" and had experienced separation anxiety each day when she went to preschool, crying upon arrival. Her mother walked her in, but Allie remained in the foyer, refusing to enter the classroom, and would sit on the floor by herself for up to four hours rather than joining the other children. Mary had tried staying at the preschool until Allie felt comfortable, but this didn't help—Allie still became distressed, and had even tried to leave the preschool by climbing the fence. Allie also experienced separation anxiety in other settings, including when cared for by a sitter, when she went to her grandparents' home, and when she attended swimming and gymnastics lessons.

In the first two sessions in which Allie was present, I had observed the interaction between the three of them and noticed that Andres repeatedly called Allie "baby" and invited her to sit on his lap when she looked to them when I asked her questions. Allie would then sit with her head on her father's chest, with her back to me. My observations from those first two sessions, together with the information Mary and Andres gave me about how they responded to Allie both at preschool and at home when her separation anxiety showed up, as well as right after she became distressed, helped me to develop my case conceptualization. Without intending to, Mary and Andres were actually *reinforcing* (i.e., making stronger) Allie's dependence on them.

Table 2 gives an overview of the six sessions with Mary and Andres (including the first two sessions that Allie attended with them).

TABLE 2. An Overview of Sessions with Mary and Andres

Session	Description	Exercises	Home Tasks
One	Case Conceptualization Let It Be	Case Conceptualization template with Mary and Andres Brainstorming what qualities and attributes Mary and Andres hoped Allie would develop Glitter bottle	Make a glitter bottle for Allie and teach her how to use it Encourage Allie to practice letting her thoughts and feelings be
Two	Let It Be Let It Go	I'm noticing that I'm feeling... I'm noticing that I'm thinking... I'm having the thought that... My mind is telling me... Thanks mind...	Develop a sticker chart for Allie focusing on joining in at preschool, gymnastics, and swimming lessons Give Allie greater independence and responsibility at preschool and home Model *let it be* and *let it go* statements to Allie
Three	Choose What Matters Do What Matters	Parenting Bull's-Eye (instead of What's in My Heart)	Discuss with Allie why she likes preschool, gymnastics, and swimming lessons Invite Allie to draw a heart (parents to write what matters inside it) Discuss with Allie what activities she could try at home (*do what matters*) Model *choose what matters* statements, then model *do what matters*

Session	Description	Exercises	Home Tasks
Four	Stay Here	Stay Here While Eating	Develop a list with the children of activities for the family to do together
			Teach the children to stay here while eating, and practice as a family
			Model *stay here* and encourage Allie to practice
Five	Notice Yourself	Watching a Movie of Your Family	Assist Allie with the Under the Sea art exercise
		Under the Sea	Use *notice yourself* statements in front of Allie
Six	Be Kind and Caring to Yourself	Write a Letter to Yourself	Use kind and caring language in front of the children
		Review of sessions and plan for Allie's first day of school	Ask the children to come up with kind and caring phrases they could use
			Ask Allie to brainstorm when she could use kind and caring phrases to speak to herself

We'll look now at each session in greater detail so you can see how I introduced Mary and Andres to each of the ACT Kidflex processes, along with *be kind and caring to yourself*, and taught them how they could teach and model them to Allie. I'll take you through our discussions, exercises used in sessions, and recommendations for home tasks.

Session One: Case Conceptualization and Let It Be

I started my first session with Allie, Mary, and Andres by developing a case conceptualization using the template shown in chapter 2. When I asked Mary and Andres if there was anything Allie was missing out on as a result of how she was managing her separation anxiety, they responded that at preschool she was missing out on having fun with her friends as well as learning. I also asked Mary and Andres if there was anything *they* were missing out on as a result of how *they* were managing Allie's separation anxiety. Mary and Andres both felt they were missing out on a lot as a couple: they were completely devoted to caring for their daughters, but they felt that they had lost their relationship and had simply become parents rather than partners. As a result, I knew that if I was able to help Allie, I'd indirectly be helping Mary and Andres too.

To get started in trying to help Allie, I asked Mary and Andres what qualities and attributes they hoped Allie would develop *(choose what matters)*. It was important to them that Allie become independent, confident, easygoing, carefree, and resilient. They also wanted Allie to be able to attend activities without distress, have sleepovers at her grandparents' home, and eventually also have sleepovers at friends' homes.

I watched the interaction between Allie and her parents and listened carefully to them, and I learned that Mary and Andres were encouraging Allie to try to avoid and also get rid of her feelings of anxiety. This isn't consistent with ACT—instead, ACT encourages letting thoughts and feelings be, rather than trying to do anything with them. As such, I realized that I also needed to give Mary and Andres some parenting strategies, rather than focusing only on treating Allie.

I felt that the first priority was to introduce Allie to *let it be*. To do this, I showed her a glitter bottle and tried to teach her to notice her thoughts and feelings without trying to do anything to get rid of them, and to let them be, but Allie was unwilling to participate in the discussion. In response, I suggested to Mary and Andres that they make a glitter bottle at home and invite Allie to choose a few different colors of glitter to generate her interest in using the glitter bottle. I suggested that they encourage Allie to look at her glitter bottle at home when she feels overwhelmed or anxious, and practice trying to let her thoughts and feelings be. I gave Mary and Andres instructions for how to make a glitter bottle and the script (see chapter 3 for the instructions and script) they could use if they wished to.

Session Two: Let It Be and Let It Go

Mary and Andres reported that they made a glitter bottle at home and used the script I gave them in the first session to teach Allie how to use it, which she was doing at home. When Mary took Allie to preschool, she reminded Allie to let her thoughts and feelings be, just like letting the glitter in the bottle be, without doing anything with them, and this was helping Allie to join her peers at preschool more quickly than previously. In this session, I recommended that Mary and Andres create a sticker chart for Allie, which I'll describe below.

Mary and Andres had identified in the first session that they wanted Allie to become more independent, which I felt would increase her self-esteem and resilience. To help Allie to become more independent, I suggested that Mary and Andres create a sticker chart to use as a reward system by drawing columns on a page for each day of the week and writing a list of behaviors they wanted Allie to engage in. After creating a chart, Mary and Andres could invite Allie to decorate it, then take her to a dollar store to purchase some stickers to select from when she did one of the behaviors on the chart. In my experience, using a sticker chart with young children can help generate their buy-in and motivation to change their own behavior, and involving the child in decorating the chart and choosing the stickers can increase their interest in the chart and the desired behaviors. If the parent is unable to access stickers, they can invite the child to do some small drawings (such as stars, hearts, flowers, or shapes) on the chart instead.

I suggested that each time Allie did one of the behaviors on the chart, Mary and Andres positively reinforce it (increasing the likelihood of the behavior continuing) by congratulating her and inviting her to choose a sticker to place on the chart. Mary and Andres chose the following behaviors for inclusion in Allie's chart: (1) walking into preschool and joining the other children without delay, and (2) joining gymnastics and swimming lessons without delay.

Instead of spending money on rewards, I recommended that Mary and Andres provide Allie with rewards that promote spending time as a family. For example, Allie could choose a board game, jigsaw puzzle, or arts and craft activity for the family to do together, or, if Mary and Andres wanted to take Allie and her two sisters out on the weekend, Allie could choose the venue, such as a park.

HELPFUL HINT

In general, it's best to help the parents come up with rewards that the child is likely to have ongoing interest in, including activities the child chooses. This will help with obtaining (and maintaining) the child's buy-in for the chart.

I also suggested that Mary and Andres create a chart for each of their other two daughters, so as not to leave them out or risk their becoming jealous or resentful of the attention Allie was receiving. Then, when the other girls earned stickers for their chart, the three girls could take turns choosing the activities for the family as their rewards.

After introducing the sticker chart, the remainder of the session focused on using *let it be* and *let it go*. I provided Mary and Andres with recommendations for how they could encourage Allie to let her thoughts of being afraid just be. I suggested that they encourage Allie to enter the preschool room when she arrives instead of sitting on her own in the foyer, even if she feels scared or worried (*let it be*), because she enjoys playing with her friends at preschool (*do what matters*). They could also ask the preschool teachers to send some of the children to greet Allie upon her arrival at preschool and to invite her to join them in an activity. I knew from Mary and Andres that once Allie joined in activities at preschool, she had a good time with her peers, so I hoped that being invited to join her peers upon arrival might help her join them more quickly.

I also suggested that Mary encourage Allie to be responsible for unpacking her bag at preschool instead of doing this for her. This was designed to help Allie become more independent, a necessary skill in order for her to receive approval from her teachers to progress to elementary school. These small steps could help empower Allie and increase her self-esteem, which may help her look forward to preschool and be more accepting of her feelings of anxiety.

Because Mary and Andres had mentioned that Allie had a very strong bond with the family dog and was very loving and protective toward him, I suggested that they also try to increase Allie's independence at home by giving her greater responsibility for the dog. Mary and Andres said that they could invite Allie to help bathe and feed their dog, and I advised them that not only was this was a great way to give Allie more responsibility, but it would also help Allie do what matters to her.

In this session, I tried to teach Allie how to use *let it be* by teaching her the phrases "I'm noticing that I'm feeling..." and "I'm noticing that I'm thinking..." However, she didn't participate, so instead I gave Mary and Andres suggestions for how they could teach Allie to let it be. I suggested that they say these phrases aloud in front of Allie and her two sisters to teach them to let their thoughts and feelings be, without having to do anything to change or avoid them. For example, Andres was nervous about public speaking and had an important presentation coming up at work. I suggested that in the lead-up to his presentation, Andres could say aloud in front of the family, "I'm noticing that I'm worried about talking in front of a large group, but I'm going to give this talk because teaching the team at work is really important to me." In this way, Andres would be showing the family that he can let his worries be, without trying to avoid or get rid of them, and he can give a talk in front of a large group even though he feels nervous (*do what matters*), because there's something about teaching his coworkers that matters to him (*choose what matters*). Then, Mary and Andres could encourage Allie to let her worries be when she arrives at preschool, and say something to herself such as *I'm noticing that I'm feeling worried, but I'm going to join the other children because I like playing with them.*

I tried to teach Allie the *let it go* process, but she didn't participate, so instead I taught Mary and Andres, using statements such as "My mind is having the thought that," and "My mind is telling me," followed by "Thanks mind" and "Thank you mind for telling me that thought." Mary, Andres, and I each took turns saying a thought our minds came up with, using "My mind is having the thought that," or "My mind is telling me," before the actual thought, followed by "Thanks mind" or "Thank you mind for telling me that thought." Then we brainstormed everyday situations where they could practice expressing their thoughts in front of their daughters, to teach the girls to let their own thoughts be and let them go. For example, Mary and Andres could say, "My mind is having the thought that I'm not sure what to cook for dinner tonight—thanks mind," or "My mind is telling me that I'm tired—thank you mind for telling me that thought."

Session Three: Choose What Matters and Do What Matters

As I was unable to engage Allie in the first two sessions, I invited Mary and Andres to attend sessions with me without Allie, which they agreed to. As a result, sessions three to six were held with Mary and Andres without Allie. In this session, Mary and Andres reported that while Allie sometimes still cried upon arrival at preschool, the time she took to join her peers had decreased significantly (to about fifteen minutes), and she was enjoying having greater independence at preschool. Allie was also joining her gymnastics and swimming lessons more quickly. At home, Allie was responding well to helping care for the family dog, and enjoying this new role. In response, her parents had given her ten stickers for her chart, and as her reward, Allie had chosen a family visit to a park.

My plan for this session was to help Mary and Andres introduce *choose what matters* to

Allie, in order to help her connect with what matters to her about preschool, gymnastics class, and swimming lessons. I invited Mary and Andres to complete the Parenting Bull's-Eye exercise to introduce them to *choose what matters*, but I let them know that I didn't recommend asking Allie to complete this exercise, as it is too complex for a five-year-old to understand. Instead, I suggested that they ask Allie why she likes going to preschool, gymnastics class, and swimming lessons, and what she might miss out on if she didn't go. Then, Mary and Andres could let Allie know that she can go to preschool, gymnastics, and swimming, even if her mind tells her that she feels worried or scared.

I suggested that after having this discussion with Allie, Mary and Andres could invite Allie to participate in a *choose what matters* drawing exercise by giving her a sheet of paper and asking her to draw or paint a heart (see chapter 4, Draw or Paint a Heart). Inside the heart, Mary or Andres could write down Allie's reasons (as Allie hadn't learned to write yet) for why she likes going to preschool, gymnastics, and swimming, and when Allie feels worried or scared about going to any of those places, Mary or Andres could suggest that Allie look at her picture, and they could read the reasons to her to remind her of what matters to her. They could also photocopy her picture and suggest that she keep it in her backpack to look at when she feels worried at preschool, gymnastics, or swimming, to remind her that those activities matter to her. I also suggested that they may wish to let her preschool teacher know about the picture in case Allie asks her teacher to read her reasons to her.

To help Allie do what matters, I recommended that Mary and Andres ask Allie if there's any activities she would like to do at home or at a local park (perhaps that she's seen her older sister do) that she hasn't done before because she felt worried or scared, for example, sports. Mary and Andres said that Allie was reluctant to try to learn to ride a bicycle, and they felt she was missing out on having fun riding with her older sister. I recommended that they try asking Allie what she might be missing out on by not learning to ride a bicycle, and whether there's anything that matters to her about bicycle riding. Then, they could suggest to Allie that she try learning to ride a bicycle, even if her mind tells her that she is afraid (let it go). If Allie is interested in learning how to ride a bicycle, her parents could add that to Allie's sticker chart to try to motivate and encourage her further.

To help teach Allie how to choose and do what matters at home, I recommended that Mary and Andres say what matters to them aloud in front of Allie and her sisters, using neutral, everyday examples, and then do these things. For example, they might say, "Exercising is important to me, so I'm going for a walk in the sunshine," then go for a walk, or "Looking after my body matters to me, so I make sure that I eat vegetables every day," then cook vegetables. Mary and Andres would be modeling to Allie and her sisters that they are choosing what matters to them and then doing what matters to them. This may remind Allie to choose what matters to her and do what matters to her, which may help her with joining in at preschool, gymnastics, swimming, and in other situations where she becomes anxious about separating from her parents (including visiting her grandparents' home and being cared for by a sitter).

Session Four: Stay Here

In this session, Mary and Andres reported that Allie was joining in more quickly at preschool, but there were still occasions when she was teary upon arrival. They also raised an issue we had discussed in the first session: that it was very important to them to spend more quality time as a couple, as well as with their children (*choose what matters*). Mary and Andres noted that they came home from work at different times and didn't eat dinner together. In this session, they decided to start eating dinner together each night, and where possible, to eat with their children.

As Mary and Andres wanted to do more activities as a family on weekends, I suggested they ask their daughters to help them develop a list of activities they'd like to do as a family, which might help obtain their buy-in and motivation.

HELPFUL HINT

Involving children in decision making is often an effective way for parents to obtain their children's buy-in and motivation.

After discussing how they could spend more time together and also as a family, I introduced Mary and Andres to *stay here* and encouraged them to practice this when they spent time together as a couple, with their children, and on their own. We also discussed ways to teach their children to stay here, which, I explained, may help Allie to manage her thoughts and feelings rather than being overwhelmed by them.

Because Mary and Andres had expressed interest in eating dinner together and as a family, I introduced *stay here* by teaching them to stay here while eating, and we did an exercise involving eating raisins to help them learn how to get started (see chapter 5 for the script for Eating While Staying Here, which you can adapt). I also suggested they try to teach their daughters to stay here while eating dinner, and I gave them a copy of the Eating Dinner with Your Family script (which you can also find in chapter 5, or on the website at http://www.newharbinger.com/49760). Mary and Andres enjoyed this exercise and agreed to try to remind the family of this *stay here* exercise on a regular basis while eating dinner.

I also recommended that Mary and Andres encourage Allie to practice staying here at preschool, gymnastics, swimming lessons, and home. For example, I suggested that they remind her, upon arrival at preschool, that she can practice staying here when playing games, doing art and crafts, and eating. I recommended that at home, Mary and Andres say statements aloud in front of Allie that remind her to stay here, such as "This flower smells beautiful" or "Look at the lovely different colors of the leaves."

Session Five: Notice Yourself

Mary and Andres advised me that Allie was now walking into preschool without distress and joining her peers immediately, and she was doing the same at swimming and gymnastics lessons. She was also managing very well when she went to her grandparents' home and when she was cared for by a sitter. Allie was also becoming more assertive at home, which Mary and Andres were pleased about, and they described her as happier, calmer, and less frustrated. These improvements were also likely to be increasing Allie's self-esteem and resilience.

In this session, I taught them the *notice yourself* process and adapted the Watching a Movie of Your Life exercise (see chapter 5 for more detail) to become "Watching a Movie of

Your Family," so they could imagine they were watching themselves, each other, and their children. When I took them through this exercise, I made sure to include behaviors that I had observed in the first two sessions when Allie was present, as well as some that Mary and Andres had informed me of. These behaviors that Mary and Andres engaged in were short-term solutions to try to manage Allie's anxiety but were not workable, long-term strategies (see chapter 2 for more detail).

I selected the following: Andres referring to Allie as "baby," Mary unpacking Allie's bag at preschool, and Mary staying at the preschool until Allie's distress settled. Even though not all of these behaviors were continuing to occur, I felt that it was still important to give Mary and Andres an opportunity to reflect on their former parenting practices in order to give them greater insight into the impact of their behaviors on their daughters. I also wanted Mary and Andres to use the ACT Kidflex strategies they were learning to use with Allie for their younger daughter, Kerry, too, to try to reduce the likelihood of reverting to the same unworkable behaviors with Kerry that they had previously used with Allie.

When Mary and Andres discussed their experiences of this exercise, they both acknowledged that their responses to Allie weren't consistent with the qualities and attributes they wanted her to develop (*choose what matters*). In response, I spent some time addressing question 11 from the case conceptualization template (see chapter 2 for more detail), "Do you think what you have been doing to manage this problem or difficulty is helping?" followed by "Does what you are doing create or cause any more problems or difficulties?" Mary and Andres both acknowledged that in trying to protect Allie from feeling anxious, they were causing her to be very dependent on them, which was the opposite of what mattered to them as parents.

I let Mary and Andres know that I didn't recommend that they invite Allie to participate in the movie exercise at home, as I felt that she'd be too young to understand it. Instead, to help Mary and Andres teach Allie the *notice yourself* process, I took them through the Under the Sea exercise (see chapter 5 for more detail). Then I gave them the script (which you can download from http://www.newharbinger.com/49 760) and suggested that for this exercise, they invite Allie to do a drawing or painting of under the sea and ask her to tell them her thoughts and feelings about going to preschool, her grandparents' home, gymnastics and swimming classes and about being cared for by a sitter. Then, on the waves she had drawn or painted, they could write the thoughts and feelings she had identified.

To remind Allie of the *notice yourself* process, I suggested that Mary and Andres say statements in front of her such as "I'm noticing that I'm really enjoying reading this book—I'll go to the library and borrow some more books."

Session Six: Be Kind and Caring to Yourself

This was my final session with Mary and Andres, who reported that Allie's anxiety had decreased significantly. She was engaging in more tasks independently, such making her bed and preparing her own breakfast, and was continuing to help care for the family dog. Not only was Allie continuing to separate from Mary easily upon arrival at preschool, but she was also separating from Mary without any hesitation or distress at her gymnastics and swimming classes, when she visited her grandparents' home, and when cared for by a sitter.

Allie's teachers also noticed this marked improvement, and they described her as much happier and more confident—and now ready to complete preschool and commence elementary school. Allie had attended orientation sessions for elementary school, which she had been excited for and thoroughly enjoyed.

I taught Mary and Andres *be kind and caring to yourself*: first teaching them how to use kind and caring language as part of their own self-talk, then inviting them to brainstorm statements they could teach to Allie to help her manage her own thoughts and feelings. I also invited Mary and

Andres to each write a kind and caring letter to themselves during the session, which they could take home and look at as a reminder of how to speak to themselves and each other with care and kindness, especially when they were worried about Allie or engaged in self-blame if Allie became anxious.

As a home task, I recommended that Mary and Andres practice expressing kind and caring self-talk in front of Allie and her sisters, to help the girls learn to speak to themselves this way. For example, they might say, "Learning how to do this is really hard for me, and I'm proud of how hard I'm trying," or "Nothing bad is going to happen to me from trying to do this task." Then, they could ask Allie and her sisters to come up with kind and caring statements to use when speaking to themselves, and encourage them to practice using them. They could also brainstorm with Allie situations where it might be helpful to use kind and caring language to speak to herself.

You'll notice that I recommended home tasks to Mary and Andres that involved them modeling the ACT Kidflex processes and *be kind and caring to yourself* to Allie and their other daughters. Even though I wasn't successful in engaging Allie in therapy, I was able to teach her parents how they could model ACT and *be kind and caring to yourself* to Allie.

As things were much improved for Allie, we agreed that this would be our final session. In reviewing the sessions, I asked Mary and Andres to identify which strategies they had found most helpful, and which ones they were continuing to use with Allie and her sisters. Interestingly, Mary and Andres reported that they were using many of the ACT Kidflex strategies in their own lives, not just for parenting Allie and her sisters. We discussed Allie's upcoming first day at elementary school and how to assist her with any associated feelings of nervousness, fear, or anxiety.

Allie commenced school a few weeks after Mary and Andres finished seeing me, and on her first day at school, her parents sent me a photo of Allie sitting in her classroom with a big smile on her face, which they were thrilled about and very proud of.

You can teach parents the ACT Kidflex and *be kind and caring to yourself* processes by looking at the family dynamics and applying them to the problem or difficulty the child is experiencing. Taking a parent through the ACT Kidflex and *be kind and caring to yourself* process helps them experience the processes themselves, and by teaching the parent how to teach and model the processes to their child, their child learns some new ways of coping. The parent can also use the ACT Kidflex processes to help their child manage their emotions, which may lead to the child's self-esteem increasing, so they become better equipped to self-soothe and, ultimately, more resilient. Once you get comfortable with the ACT Kidflex processes, you'll notice that the language you use with parents is largely similar; it's just the details that change according to the specific problem or difficulty. In this way, the ACT Kidflex is applicable for a wide range of issues.

Conclusion

You have completed working with the child's parent(s) and addressed the processes of the ACT Kidflex with them, as well as *be kind and caring to yourself*. Parents can use the home tasks that you recommended to practice their own use of the ACT Kidflex and *be kind and caring to yourself* processes, and also to teach their child (as well as their other children) and show them how to use the processes to manage their problem or difficulty. In the next chapter, we'll conclude with some tips on how you can start using what you've learned in this book.

CHAPTER 8

Final Tips for Using ACT with Children

In this book you've learned the six processes of the ACT Kidflex *(let it be, let it go, choose what matters, do what matters, stay here,* and *notice yourself)* as well as *be kind and caring to yourself.* You've also learned how to use ACT to work with parents in situations where their child doesn't attend therapy. So now it's time for you to get started in implementing what you've read in this book. It's important to start trying these techniques straight away, while they're fresh in your mind. My own experience has been that when I learn new ACT techniques and exercises and start using them within a few days, they become integral parts of my toolkit, and I continue to use them over time. Let's look at some tips for how to start using what you've learned.

Practice On Yourself First

The best person to practice what you've learned in this book on is yourself. In case you're wondering where in the ACT Kidflex to begin, I recommend that you revisit chapters 3, 4, and

5 and make a list of the techniques and exercises for each process in the ACT Kidflex that resonate most with you, or that you're curious about or keen to try. Then, you can revisit chapter 6 *(be kind and caring to yourself)* and make a list for that too. Afterward, read through your lists and try one exercise per process per day (you can try more than one process per day if you're ambitious), until you've tried all the exercises on your list. I recommend following the same order in which the processes are presented in this book, starting with *let it be* and *let it go*. When you're ready to start using ACT with children, your list may become a helpful resource.

By first trying the exercises and techniques yourself before using them with children, you'll get to experience firsthand how using them can feel. This will give you greater insight, the ability to share with children your own experiences of doing the exercises and techniques (using appropriate disclosure), as well as a stronger basis for answering their questions. In turn, you'll have greater credibility as a therapist, which may also help you build rapport with the child.

Learning ACT and becoming proficient in its use definitely takes time, and the more you can practice and use ACT in your own life, the better you'll become at teaching it to the children you work with. I encourage you to practice the exercises in this book, and if you find any of them difficult, try them again the next day. It may take you some time to feel comfortable and confident using ACT: that's okay, and is to be expected. When trying these exercises yourself the first few times, you might notice your mind telling you that you're doing them wrong, or that you feel awkward, or that you'll never get the hang of them. Please be reassured that that's a very common experience, especially for therapists who are new to using ACT. You can notice those thoughts and thank your mind for them, and any others it cares to share with you. You can also let yourself know that you're trying your best and that learning new exercises is hard for many therapists. Then you can keep going with your practice. Once you've tried the exercises yourself, then you'll be ready to try out what you've learned with children and their parents.

It's Okay to Model Imperfection

Modeling imperfection to the children you work with, and showing them that we don't have to do everything perfectly, is really valuable teaching. It also demonstrates your own use of flexibility (remember that the goal of the ACT Kidflex is *I am flexible*). An important part of developing your own style of ACT involves making mistakes in order to work out how you want to deliver exercises to children, and perhaps adapt them and create your own. When you show children that you're willing to—and in fact *do*—make mistakes, you also demonstrate your own authenticity. So, if your mind tells you that you need to be really great at ACT, or much better at it before you'll be ready to start using the ACT Kidflex with children, take a moment to think about why using ACT with children matters to you, and then get started.

Keep Your Language Simple

In writing this book, my greatest hope was that I'd inspire you to use ACT with children aged five to twelve years. You'll have noticed throughout the book that everything is presented in simple and developmentally appropriate language, using easy-to-relate-to examples, with recommendations for home tasks based on day-to-day activities. I recommend that if you wish to modify the exercises in this book, just make slight modifications, and make sure that you keep your language and examples simple and developmentally appropriate based on your clients. Otherwise, the child might not understand what you've taught them and then be unlikely to know how to practice in between sessions, self-soothe, and make changes to their coping strategies. This also applies to giving recommendations to parents.

Slow Down

One very common mistake therapists make when learning ACT is trying to introduce too many ACT processes, techniques, examples, and exercises in the same session. I recommend that you slow down, and don't try to introduce the child to too much in the one session, as they will retain more when processes are fully explained and explored in depth. One of the things I've found really helpful is to practice noticing myself in sessions, and if I find that I'm trying to introduce too much—by giving the child or their parents lots of examples, or by introducing too many exercises—then I pause and slow down. To help yourself slow down, you could write yourself a plan, in advance, for the child's next session that includes the techniques, examples, and exercises for the ACT Kidflex process(es) you want to introduce them to. If you find in sessions that you're going too fast but are concerned that you won't finish teaching the child the process (or processes), that's okay; you can continue using the same process in the next session—remember, you don't have to only spend one session per process. You can also revisit the same process again in future sessions if you identify a need to.

Parting Words

Working with children can be a very rewarding experience as you are providing your young clients with life-enhancing tools they can continue to use as they grow into adolescents and adults. It can also be exciting and fun. I find that using the ACT Kidflex is very effective because it's been designed to be simple and developmentally appropriate for treating children aged five to twelve years. If you aren't working with children at the moment, you can use many of the techniques, examples, and exercises in this book with adolescent or adult clients too—just adapt any examples or exercises as you need to. And even if you aren't working with clients at the moment, you can still reap many benefits from practicing on yourself and implementing ACT in your own life.

Now that you've finished reading this book, please go to the book's website, http://www.ne wharbinger.com/49760, to read my extended case protocol—a session-by-session guide showing you how I worked with an eight-year-old child using ACT and *be kind and caring to yourself*. The protocol shows how I taught each process of the ACT Kidflex, the exercises I used, and recommendations I provided to both the child and her parents. On the website, you'll also find all of the book's worksheets in color for download, the case conceptualization template, and some scripts of exercises to give to parents.

I hope this book has inspired you and given you some useful, new tools. I wish you every success in your ACT journey.

References

Baer, D.M., Wolf, M.M., & Risley, T.R. (1968). Some current dimensions of applied behavior analysis. *Journal of Applied Behavior Analysis, 1(1),* 91–97.

Barnes-Holmes, D., Barnes-Holmes, Y., McHugh, L., & Hayes, S.C. (2004). Relational frame theory: Some implications for understanding and treating human psychopathology. *International Journal of Psychology and Psychological Therapy, 4,* 355–375.

Beck, A.T., Rush, A., Shaw, B.F., & Emery, G. (1979). *Cognitive therapy of depression.* Guilford Press.

Bell, T., Montague, J., Elander, J., & Gilbert, P.(2019). 'A definite feel-it moment': Embodiment, externalization and emotion during chair-work in compassion-focused therapy. *Counselling and Psychotherapy Research,* 1–20.

Biglan, A., & Hayes, S.C. (1996). Should the behavioral sciences become more pragmatic? The case for functional contextualism in research on human behavior. *Applied & Preventive Psychology, 5,* 47–57.

Black. T.D. (2016). *A comparison of acceptance and commitment therapy and cognitive behavioural therapy for enhancing adolescent mental health within school curricula.* [Thesis submitted for the award of Doctor of Philosophy]. Monash University.

Bluth, K. (2017). *The self-compassion workbook for teens.* New Harbinger Publications.

Brock, M.J., Batten, S.V., Walser, R.D., & Robb, H.B. (2015). Recognizing common clinical mistakes in ACT: A quick analysis and call to awareness. *Journal of Contextual Behavioral Science, 4,* 139–143.

Coyne, L.W. (2011). *Using ACT with children, adolescents and parents: Getting experiential in family work.* [Two day workshop]. Australian Psychological Society Child, Adolescent and Family Psychology Interest Group, Adelaide, South Australia, Australia.

Coyne, L.W., McHugh, L., & Martinez, E.R. (2011). Acceptance and commitment therapy (ACT): Advances and applications with children, adolescents, and families. *Child Adolescent Psychiatry Clinics of North America, 20(2),* 379–399.

Coyne, L.W., & Murrell, A.R. (2009). *The joy of parenting: An acceptance and commitment therapy guide to effective parenting in the early years.* New Harbinger Publications.

Dahl, J., & Lundgren, T. (2006). *Living beyond your pain living beyond your pain: Using acceptance & commitment therapy to ease chronic pain.* New Harbinger Publications.

De Shazer, S. (1988). *Clues: Investigating solutions in brief therapy.* W.W. Norton & Company.

Fang, S., & Ding, D. (2020). A meta-analysis of the efficacy of acceptance and commitment therapy for children. *Journal of Contextual Behavioral Science, 15,* 225–234.

Gilbert, P. (2009). *The compassionate mind.* Constable.

Greco, L., & Emery, D. (2010). *ACT in family & school settings.* [Conference session]. Association for Contextual Behavioral Science (ACBS) Australian and New Zealand Chapter, Conference, Adelaide, South Australia, Australia.

Greenberg, L.S., Rice, L.N., & Elliott, R. (1993). *Facilitating emotional change: The Moment-by-moment process.* The Guilford Press.

Greenberg, L.S., & Watson, J.C. (2006). *Emotion-focused therapy for depression.* American Psychological Association.

Harris, R. (2007). *The happiness trap. Exisle Publishing.*

Harris, R. (2009). *ACT made simple: An easy-to-read primer on acceptance and commitment therapy.* New Harbinger Publications.

Harris, R. (2019). *ACT made simple: An easy-to-read primer on acceptance and commitment therapy* (2nd ed.). New Harbinger Publications.

Hayes, L. (2011). *Workshop on ACT with young people.* Melbourne, Victoria, Australia.

Hayes, S.C. (1993). Analytic goals and the varieties of scientific contextualism. In S.C. Hayes, L.J. Hayes, H.W. Reese, & T.R. Sarbin (Eds.), *Varieties of scientific contextualism* (pp. 11–27). Context Press.

Hayes, S.C., Barnes-Holmes, D., & Roche, B. (Eds.) (2001). *Relational frame theory: A post Skinnerian account of human language and cognition.* Kluwer Academic/Plenum Publications.

Hayes, S.C., Hayes, L.J., & Reese, H.W. (1988). Finding the philosophical core: A review of Stephen C. Pepper's World Hypotheses. *Journal of the Experimental Analysis of Behavior, 50,* 97–111.

Hayes, S.C., Luoma, J.B., Bond, F.W., Masuda, A., & Lillis, J. (2006). Acceptance and commitment therapy: Model, processes and outcomes. *Behavior Research and Therapy, 44,* 1–25.

Hayes, S.C., Pistorello, J., & Levin, M.E. (2012). Acceptance and commitment therapy as a unified model of behavior change. *The Counselling Psychologist, 40(7),* 976–1002.

Hayes, S.C., & Smith, S. (2005). *Get out of your mind & into your life.* New Harbinger Publications.

Hayes, S.C., Strosahl, K.D., & Wilson, K.G. (1999). *Acceptance and commitment therapy.* Guilford Press.

Hayes, S.C., Strosahl, K.D., & Wilson, K.G. (2012). *Acceptance and commitment therapy: The process and practice of mindful change* (2nd ed.). Guilford Press.

Hofmann, S.G., & Smits, J.A. (2008). Cognitive-behavioral therapy for adult anxiety disorders: A meta-analysis of randomized placebo-controlled trials. *Journal of Clinical Psychiatry, 69* (4), 621–632.

Kolts, R.L. (2016). *CFT made simple.* New Harbinger Publications.

Luoma, J.B., Hayes, S.C., & Walser, R.D. (2007). *Learning ACT.* New Harbinger Publications.

Neff, K., & Germer, C. (2018). *The mindful self-compassion workbook.* The Guilford Press.

Neuberger, J. (1999). Let's do away with "patients." *British Medical Journal, 318,* 1756–8.

Rafaeli, E., Bernstein, D.P., & Young, J. (2011). *Schema therapy: Distinctive features.* Routledge.

Roediger, E., Stevens, B.A., & Brockman, R. (2018). *Contextual schema therapy.* Context Press.

Saltzman, A., & Goldin, P. (2008). Mindfulness-based stress reduction for school-age children. In L.A. Greco & S.C. Hayes (Eds.), *Acceptance and mindfulness treatments for children & adolescents* (pp.139–161). New Harbinger Publications.

Simon, A., & Garfunkel, P. (1964). *Wednesday morning 3AM.* [Album]. Columbia Records.

Strosahl, K.D. (2015). *Brief interventions for radical change: The essentials of focused acceptance and commitment therapy* [Conference session]. Association for Contextual Behavioral Science Southeast Chapter Conference, Lafayette, Louisiana, United States.

Swain, J., Hancock, K., Dixon, A., & Bowman, J. (2015). Acceptance and commitment therapy for children: A systematic review of intervention studies. *Journal of Contextual Behavioral Science, 4* (2), 73–85.

Twohig, M.P. (2014). Two-day workshop on ACT for anxiety disorders [Conference session]. Association for Contextual Behavioral Science Australia and New Zealand Chapter Annual Conference, Sunshine Coast, Queensland, Australia.

Twohig, M.P., Abramowitz, J.S., Smith, B.M., Fabricant, L.E., Jacoby, R.J., Morrison, K.L., Bluett, E.J., Reuman, L., Blakey, S.M., & Ledermann, T. (2018). Adding acceptance and commitment therapy to exposure and response prevention for obsessive-compulsive disorder: A randomized controlled trial. *Behavior Research and Therapy*, *108*, 1–9.

Twohig, M.P., Hayes, S.C., & Berlin, K.S. (2008). A behavioral approach to cognitions: Acceptance and commitment therapy for childhood externalizing disorders. In L.A. Greco & S.C. Hayes (Eds.), *Acceptance and mindfulness interventions for children, adolescents, and families* (pp.164–186). New Harbinger Publications.

Wilson, K. (2008). *Mindfulness for two*. New Harbinger Publications.

Tamar D. Black, PhD, is an educational and developmental psychologist in Melbourne, Victoria, Australia. She is a school psychologist, and runs a private practice working with children, adolescents, young adults, and parents. She has extensive experience providing clinical supervision to early-career and highly experienced psychologists. She also provides training in acceptance and commitment therapy (ACT) to clinicians and teachers in using ACT with children and adolescents, and using ACT in schools.

Foreword writer **Russ Harris** is a therapist and coach, and was a general practitioner before being introduced to ACT. Russ is a world-renowned ACT trainer, and is author of *ACT Made Simple, The Happiness Trap, The Reality Slap, ACT with Love,* and more.

Real change *is* possible

For more than forty-five years, New Harbinger has published proven-effective self-help books and pioneering workbooks to help readers of all ages and backgrounds improve mental health and well-being, and achieve lasting personal growth. In addition, our spirituality books offer profound guidance for deepening awareness and cultivating healing, self-discovery, and fulfillment.

Founded by psychologist Matthew McKay and Patrick Fanning, New Harbinger is proud to be an independent, employee-owned company. Our books reflect our core values of integrity, innovation, commitment, sustainability, compassion, and trust. Written by leaders in the field and recommended by therapists worldwide, New Harbinger books are practical, accessible, and provide real tools for real change.

 **newharbinger**publications

- **Free e-booklets of the most popular** *Quick Tips for Therapists*
- **Surveys on book topics you'd like to see us publish,** and resources you're looking for to better serve your clients

Join the New Harbinger Clinicians Club today at newharbinger.com/clinicians-club

Check out our ever-growing course catalog and find the training that's right for you.

CONCEPTUAL | EXPERIENTIAL | PRACTICAL

Did you know there are **free tools** you can download for this book?

Free tools are things like **worksheets**, **guided meditation exercises**, and **more** that will help you get the most out of your book.

You can download free tools for this book—whether you bought or borrowed it, in any format, from any source—from the New Harbinger website. All you need is a NewHarbinger.com account. Just use the URL provided in this book to view the free tools that are available for it. Then, click on the "download" button for the free tool you want, and follow the prompts that appear to log in to your NewHarbinger.com account and download the material.

You can also save the free tools for this book to your **Free Tools Library** so you can access them again anytime, just by logging in to your account! Just look for this button on the book's free tools page.

+ Save this to my free tools library

If you need help accessing or downloading free tools, visit **newharbinger.com/faq** or contact us at **customerservice@newharbinger.com**.

Back Cover Material

A Comprehensive ACT Guide for Treating Kids Ages 5 to 12

If you treat children with mental health conditions such as depression or anxiety, you know that interventions designed for adults often do not work with younger clients. What you need is a developmentally appropriate treatment plan to help kids regulate intense emotions and cope with life's challenges. Grounded in acceptance and commitment therapy (ACT), the approach outlined in this professional guide is practical and easy to implement in sessions, and includes skills that are simple enough for children to use on their own in day-to-day life—whether at home, in school, or out in the world.

.

"A beautifully written and comprehensive book that addresses every aspect of the use of ACT methods with children."
—STEVEN C. HAYES, PhD, originator of acceptance and commitment therapy (ACT)

ACT for Treating Children offers a customized adaptation of the ACT Hexaflex—a key component of ACT—called the ACT *Kidflex* to help young clients build resilience and psychological flexibility. You'll find detailed case studies, transcripts, activities, experiential exercises, worksheets, and session plans to help children manage emotions. Finally, you'll find strategies for involving parents in treatment when appropriate, and enlisting them as "ACT coaches" in the child's therapy. Whether you're a seasoned ACT clinician or new to ACT, this go-to guide has everything you need to help kids thrive!

TAMAR D. BLACK, PhD, is an educational and developmental psychologist in Melbourne, Victoria, Australia. She is a school psychologist and runs a private practice, working with children, adolescents, young adults and parents.

A

about this book, *2, 4, 6*
acceptance and commitment therapy (ACT), *6, 7*
  case conceptualization process in, *51, 52, 53, 55, 57, 59, 60, 62, 64, 66, 68, 70, 72, 73, 75, 77, 79, 81, 83, 84*
  CBT distinguished from, *7, 9*
  conveying voluntary nature of, *91, 93*
  exposure response therapy with, *177, 178, 180, 182, 184, 185, 187*
  imaginary lenses worn in, *47, 49, 51*
  introducing to children, *84, 85, 87, 89, 91, 93*
  learning to use, *36, 38*
  practicing the techniques of, *35, 36, 327, 329*

  relational frame theory and, *9*
  suitability for children, *11, 13, 14*
  therapeutic stance in, *26, 27, 29, 31, 33, 35, 36*
ACT Hexaflex, *14*
ACT Kidflex, *14, 16, 18, 20, 21, 23, 26*
  being kind and caring to yourself and, *246, 248, 250*
  description and illustration of, *14, 16*
  goal of, *23, 26, 149, 237, 291, 294, 329*
  how to use, *97, 98*
  linking processes of, *189, 191, 215*
  overview of processes in, *16, 18, 20, 21, 23*
  practicing on yourself, *327, 329*
  training parents in, *287, 325*

9 781038 758781